WHY WE DON'T SUCK

ALSO BY DENIS LEARY

WHY WE SUCK: A FEEL GOOD GUIDE TO STAYING
FAT, LOUD, LAZY AND STUPID

SUCK ON THIS YEAR: LYFAO @ 140 CHARACTERS OR LESS

WHY WE DON'T SUCK

AND HOW ALL OF US NEED TO STOP BEING SUCH PARTISAN LITTLE BITCHES

DR. DENIS LEARY

CROWN ARCHETYPE
NEW YORK

Copyright © 2017 by Denis Leary

All rights reserved.
Published in the United States by Crown Archetype,
an imprint of the Crown Publishing Group,
a division of Penguin Random House LLC, New York.
crownpublishing.com

Crown Archetype and colophon is a registered trademark
of Penguin Random House LLC.

Library of Congress Cataloging-in-Publication Data
is available upon request.

ISBN 978-1-5247-6273-5
Ebook ISBN 978-1-5247-6275-9

PRINTED IN THE UNITED STATES OF AMERICA

Maps on pages 135–38 © Dr. Jack Grieve
Jacket design by Rachel Willey
Jacket photograph by Jill Greenberg

10 9 8 7 6 5 4 3 2 1

First Edition

There's no room for demons when you're self-possessed.

—CARRIE FISHER

WARNING

They have something called Sensitive Readers now. Publishers hire them to comb through each page of a new manuscript looking for words, phrases, and ideas that are currently deemed politically incorrect and therefore capable of upsetting their delicate lives.

Two of them were placed under medical care while trying to finish this book.

AUTHOR'S NOTE

Every fact in this book was Googled and double-Googled. Then Googled again. Except for the facts that came from my voluminous but sometimes cloudy collection of memories. If you don't believe they happened, you can kiss my Irish ass. This is how I remember them happening. Some names have been changed to protect the innocent.

Although I don't know why. Because in the end—just like me— they are all guilty.

I should also remind you that I'm a doctor. A real doctor. Of arts and letters. I have the official diploma that says so hanging in my office. There's a photo of it in my first book.

How did I become a doctor?

I got famous.

So my alma mater, Emerson College, from which I actually graduated in 1979, gave me an honorary doctorate many years later when I became a movie star. I made a very funny and extremely short speech, which the kids loved because they were graduating and wanted to go party their asses off.

Emerson saved my life. First by giving me a scholarship, which was the only way I could ever afford to attend college. And then by virtue of its teachers, who created an atmosphere that allowed creative students in the arts to thrive.

I also met my wife, Ann, there.

And we are living happily ever after.

Anyway, the point is: I'm a doctor. So I obviously know what the hell I'm talking about. And if I make fun of you in this book, it's for good reason. I also make fun of myself in here. A lot. Like, a fuck of a lot.

So look at the bright side: we both deserve it.

Plus, if you sue me, it'll just sell more copies of the book and even MORE people will end up reading whatever it is that's got you in a snit. My prescription? Lighten up and laugh a little. And if you can't manage that? This is REALLY gonna suck for you.

Dedicated to my wife, Ann—who is everything.

Let he who is without sin cast the first stone. I'm gonna throw these fuckin' eggs.

—DENIS LEARY, 1971

SHORTEST OPENING
CHAPTER EVER

I was sitting in the Miss Worcester Diner with my dad one day in 1965 when the guy behind the counter delivered my cheeseburger and said to him, "John, is there anything you can't do? Some guys who come in here say you're the best mechanic they ever worked with, other guys say as a carpenter and electrician you could pretty much build your own house. On top of which you play a great accordion, and I hear you were a pretty goddamned fast man on the Gaelic football field both over in Ireland and right around the corner here in Crompton Park. But if someone asked you to pick one thing and say that's what you are, how would you answer?"

My dad looked up from his coffee and said, "An American."

If you're going through hell, keep on going.

—WINSTON CHURCHILL

Lead, follow, or get the fuck out of my way.

—GENERAL GEORGE S. PATTON

OH SAY CAN YOU SCREAM

Dear Hillary supporters: What happened? Michigan, Wisconsin, and Pennsylvania is what happened. Plus, a server wiped so clean it might as well have been a free ad for BleachBit. How much do bridal party yoga pants cost? Three fucking states.

But look at the bright side: It wasn't the end of the world.

Trump was victorious. And one year later the sky hasn't fallen, the sun still rises, and Cher didn't move to Canada. Plus, Canada's not building a wall to keep US out.

Yet.

There will be no Trumpageddon. Or Hillary Apology Tour.

Dear Trump supporters: Despite what your hero says, the press is not the enemy of the American people. The real enemy of the American people is butter—and politicians who have no sense of humor. Too many of us have turned into chubby fast-food junkies who can't take a fucking joke.

The president is guilty on both counts.

And no matter how many misspelled tweets and blabbermouth declarations he makes, there was no voter fraud or Yugest Inauguration Crowd Ever Seen.

Period.

And Trump won't be impeached for election ambiguities or for damaging the ozone with a massive carbon footprint comprised mostly of hair spray. It's very simple math: the House of Representatives can't agree on a catered lunch, never mind removing the president.

Democrats moan, Republicans groan. Hillary speaks, the president tweets. Leaving people like me to ask the really important questions, like: Whatever happened to covfefe-flavored covfefe?

American politics has always been a clown show, but our latest presidential circus finished as a fifty-fifty proposition that left this country divided right down the middle. Trump's hyperpatriotic motto "MAKE AMERICA GREAT AGAIN!" resonated with one-half of the population. The rest bought into the ultrabland "HILLARY FOR AMERICA!" They both promised to bring back manufacturing jobs.

Which will all be done by robots within the next seven years.

And this clowniest of all clown shows ended up with no clowning at all. Funny friends I love from both sides of the aisle have lost their minds and all attempts at humor as they rage-tweet against Republicans or tweet-brag at the Democrats in a nonstop series of social media insult bombs. Hillary and Trump are both infected by the unfunny flu. Now they're coming to get the rest of us. But not on my fucking watch.

#MakeAmericaLaughAgain

Fake News: Trump won in a landslide.

Alternative Fact: Hillary handed him a last-minute squeaker.

Trump promised to drain the swamp. He didn't. He just filled it up to overflowing with rich friends and family members. Just like Hillary would have done. And each tribe still drenches our electronic devices on a weekly basis, continuing the political turmoil with ridiculous partisan bullshit.

Chelsea Clinton tries to tell Republicans-at-large that she doesn't care about money. After a three-million-dollar wedding to a hedge fund founder. Eric Trump says Democrats aren't even people—unless they play golf on Trump-owned courses, I'm guessing. Because Eric's only real contribution to society so far is knowing the difference between a nine iron and a lob wedge. And how much to charge you for using both.

#MakeAmericaGolfAgain

Meanwhile, nothing gets done in D.C. They hold hearings to form committees to figure out sound bites to get book deals and fatter lobbying funds. They're not fighting for us, they're fighting for TV time—and free filet mignon.

And what are the actual voters doing? We're worried about Russian wiretaps on our Chinese phones while driving Japanese cars made in Mexico and sipping Guatemalan lattes topped off with Canadian milk.

#MakeAmericaAnxiousAgain

Trump puts a tanning bed in the Lincoln Bedroom. Hillary gets paid for making speeches about why she isn't sleeping there. While I'm still trying to decipher exactly what her motto was supposed to mean. "HILLARY FOR AMERICA"? She would have been better off with a more truthful approach: "HEY, AMERICA—IT'S MY FUCKING TURN!"

Trump won with 306 electoral college votes, finishing forty-fifth out of the fifty-eight presidential elections in American history. Most high-ranking civil servants would shy away from discussing such pedestrian results and humbly enter office hoping to change people's minds with four years of positive bipartisan action.

Not The Donald.

He decided to ignore the math and manufacture fantasy figures about My Amazing Victory and My Large Electoral College Numbers and The Biggest Mandate Ever. Can you really trust this man when he says, "I guarantee there's no problem," regarding the size of his own penis? Forget Billy Bush and "grab 'em by the pussy." Here's some REAL locker room talk: guys with big cocks don't boast about them.

They're too busy fucking.

Meanwhile, how insane is it that our most recent round of presidential debates devolved into a discussion about the girth and length of a male candidate's genitalia? Let me speak for every guy I know—from both ends of the political spectrum—when I say this in a VERY bipartisan voice:

Ewwwww.

And let me publicly record the reaction of every woman I know from age nineteen to ninety:

EWWWWWWWWWW!

If we ever needed proof that it's time for a woman to lead this country, Marco Rubio and Donald Trump provided it live one night on national TV when they both acted like fourteen-year-old boys at a circle jerk. I'm surprised Carly Fiorina's head didn't explode. Can you imagine her beginning a debate by saying, "The education budget is tight and so is my vagina"?

No.

The only recorded instance of Carly discussing her breasts in public was to warn other women about early cancer detection. While Trump and Rubio aimed street-corner crotch arrows at each other, Carly was focused on real issues, whether you agreed with her or not.

So clearly one would think much of America was primed for a smart, classy, female voice speaking into its most powerful public microphone. And former Secretary of State Clinton seemed to have that bull by the horns. Two weeks before November 8 she held what looked like an insurmountable lead. Part of which actually held up, because Hillary won the popularity portion of the contest by almost three million votes.

Which is probably how many e-mails she erased during the course of her campaign.

If you're a Hillary fan or an extreme die-hard liberal, stop reading this book right now. It's only going to melt your lefty gossamer wings. Go buy Elizabeth Warren's new book: *I May Look Like Annette Bening, But I'm Really a Native American*. It'll teach you how to pay higher taxes while quoting Rosa Parks.

If you're a Trump fan or an extreme-right-wing conservative, close this book and put it back on the shelf *immédiatement* (that's French for "now"). 'Cause otherwise your sanctimonious Second Amendment toes will curl up and pretty soon you are gonna be wicked fuckin' pissed (that's Boston for "angry").

Go to the current affairs and politics section of the bookstore, which is where you should find something to soothe your soul. Like the latest edgy Ann Coulter book that might as well be titled *Democrats Can Suck My Dick*.

By the way, I bet Ann's dick is bigger than both Donald's and Hillary's combined. Like her or not, Ann doesn't take shit from anyone. I wish Bill O'Reilly had placed a midnight masturbation call to Coulter. His cock would still be stuck in a No Spin Zone.

If you're holding a hardcover copy of this book or perusing it on an iPad or your smartphone, it's late 2017 or early 2018 and America remains the greatest country on earth. If you're watching these words fly through the air on the new Apple iGram (their Hologram Launchpad Device), it's 2028 and some of you are probably still flipping out about what a popular-vote drubbing Senator Jon Stewart and Congressman Stephen Colbert just took from President-elect Dwayne Johnson and Vice President Joe Piscopo, even after all those lurid stories broke about Joe banging The Rock's seventeen-year-old babysitter.

But all was seemingly forgiven when Joe did his hilarious throwback Sinatra impression as he guest-hosted *SNL* the weekend before Election Day. Referencing the May-December relationship during a parody version of "My Way"—with twenty-two-year-old cast member Suri Jolie-Pitt-McConaughey-Cruise playing the object of his affection—the former New Jersey governor slayed on social media with members of Generation Y's Second Wave Millennials.

In retrospect it's clear the country was due to go Republican again after eight years of Elaine Benes. But the good news is that ex-President Louis-Dreyfus will soon return to HBO and star in a half-hour comedy series written and created by her former second in command, Vice President Larry David.

And even though all he did was play golf for almost two full terms—establishing a probably never-to-be-broken Guinness World Record for Most Consecutive Days Playing a Sport (2,837)—David deserves our thanks for stepping in to take over after Bernie Sanders went off the rails with his Free Health Care for Former ISIS Members proposal in March 2021.

President Rock, whose famed campaign slogan **#ChiselMeIn** really caught fire, has sworn to uphold his promise to change the spelling of "America" on day one of his new administration, officially replacing the *e* with a *u*.

President Trump—who was forced to resign from office after admitting his Trump ties were made by Chinese orphans paid in organic rice balls ("This isn't some cheap rice out of an Uncle Ben's box, folks. I hear it's the best-tasting rice in the world!")—praised President Rock's victory on his hit Trump Network TV show *Big League, Big Hands,* while gifting each audience member a free photo of himself and fourth wife Hailey Baldwin.

Meanwhile, Melania's controversial 2019 deportation by Donald made news again after New York City mayor Chelsea Clinton welcomed the ex–first lady back to the United States during Fashion Week, only to find out her father, Bill, was accused of groping several models during the show, which stole the media spotlight from the release of Hillary's latest best-selling book, *Orange Is the New Electoral College: My Prison Epiphanies.*

Sound ridiculous? Not anymore.

What may have played out like political science fiction a scant twelve months ago now seems to be a foreseeable future. This is what happens when Amuricans have such limited alternatives.

Last year, if you asked me the famous "who do you want answering the White House phone at three o'clock in the morning" question, my response would've been immediate: Not Bill Clinton. While he's getting blown by another pudgy intern. And no more members of the Bush family. Especially ones not named George. What the hell kind of name is Jeb? Sounds like a jar of discount fucking peanut butter. He should've copped that old advertising catchphrase for his campaign motto: "Choosy conservatives choose Jeb!"

I agree with what David Letterman once said: "Bush presidencies are like the *Godfather* films: you're better off stopping after two."

I've had enough of the Clintons and the Bushes, the same faces and arguments for the last three decades. Forget hope and change—what happened to choices? In a country where you can buy sixty-seven different flavors of ice cream, binge-watch 435 TV shows, and customize your morning coffee until it's actually just another flavor of ice cream, how is it we only get two political parties to pick from?

This year, having blown through eight bazillion dollars and sixteen months of televised screaming, we were left with these two options: an apricot-colored guy who occasionally refers to himself as Ratings Machine DJT, and a woman who must own more pants than Men's Fucking Wearhouse.

Hillary reminds me of an angry math nun I had in seventh grade. So every time she began bellowing out another stilted speech on TV, my spine would harden like I forgot to do my homework. And whenever she managed to lower her humorless voice to its Nurse Ratched register, I turned into Jack Nicholson in *One Flew Over the Cuckoo's Nest:* it just made me wanna piss her off even more. Hillary's patronizing Missile of Shame launchpad approach often backfired. The basket of deplorables were already supporting Donald, but a lot of undecided voters were turned off by her lecturous indignation. Hard to be smug when you sound like a seagull.

That's not sexism, folks. It's nunism.

Then she would go on *Ellen* or *Fallon* or some other breezy talk show and be charmingly relaxed with a sunshiny smile and a happy disposition.

What. The. Fuck.

You can count on half of one hand the times Trump has actually laughed out loud in public. Once on *Fallon* when Jimmy mussed up the astonishing mound of chemical products that hold his head in place, and once more at the annual Al Smith Dinner when Hillary zinged him with some great one-liners. He certainly wasn't smiling when Obama and Seth Meyers peppered him comically at the 2011 White House Correspondents' Dinner. His skin was so thin you could practically see his Big Mac brain stem vowing revenge. It was a joy to observe. Like a scientific experiment in pomposity.

I love watching Trump deal with descending the stairs of *Air Force One.* THAT'S a true laugh jackpot. He looks like a timid toddler every single time—eyes glued to his feet as if he's just downed a stolen bottle of Tia Maria and didn't know he had to exit the aircraft. Watch his process whenever he deplanes:

1. Stand stock-still.
2. Quickly wave to whoever the fuck.
3. Stare down and pray: *Left foot, right foot.* Repeat.
4. *EYES DOWN! DON'T LEAN TOO FAR FORWARD! WE CAN DO THIS!*

Each time he reaches ground level the sense of relief is deafening. Check the *Access Hollywood* tape. The disgusting misogyny grenade overshadowed his concern about exiting that bus. He stood at the top of the stairs, paused for a moment, and said, "It's always good if you don't fall out of the bus. Like Gerald Ford, remember?" Then he took a deep breath, stared down, and began to gingerly move his worried white feet.

It's nice to know our tough-talking president will elbow jab his way to the front of a G7 summit meeting, fire disloyal cabinet members face-to-face, and put down the press in person with an explosive confidence never seen before.

As long as there ain't any stairs involved.

That's probably why he took the escalator down into the lobby of Trump Tower when announcing his campaign: staircases are Donald Trump's kryptonite.

#MakeEscalatorsMandatory

Meanwhile, right from the get-go, I dug his off-the-cuff approach to public speaking. It's like a comedy roller coaster every time he talks. Full of spastic elastic Jim Carrey facial takes and loudmouth meanderings your drunk uncle might spout at a boozed-up summer barbecue:

"Do I approve of waterboarding? You bet your ass I do."

"And you can tell them to go FUCK themselves!"

"I would bomb the shit out of 'em!"

Full disclosure: I've said the exact same stuff without being drunk but with at least one "motherfucker" tossed into every sentence. Then again, I'm not the leader of the free world right now.

I love watching President Trump boast about how great/successful/rich he is, probably because it makes me feel like such a good/humble/nice person by comparison. He's called himself smart so many times even Fredo would throw a red flag. You know who makes Donald Trump look smart? Donald Trump Jr. Stick him in a room with a bowlful of Skittles and some Russian spies and pretty soon you start to resemble Neil deGrasse Tyson. Who might be the only famous person President Trump hasn't insulted yet. He's a bipartisan bulldozer. He's a Monster Truck Ego Show, which makes fascinating television. It's like the WWE took over the West Wing. Donald is Hulk Hogan with more hair, no steroids, and no script: just grab the mike and bloviate.

His free-association bully pulpit approach becomes a relentless me, myself, and I gasconade. Whenever he puts his unchained id on public display, it bounces from subject to subject faster than an Alzheimer's outpatient. Imagine his set list if he planned it out in advance: Big Hands, Bad Hombres, Schwarzenegger's Ratings, Build a Wall, Disgusting Rosie, Where's My African American?

It's a political car crash you can't look away from.

But when you give Donald a printed speech and force him to

say it word-by-word? Suddenly he has less charisma than Chuck Schumer's left ball.

#WhatTheFuck

Listen, if you're not a gifted elocutionist like Ronald Reagan, Bill Clinton, or Barack Obama, what makes you think reading aloud from a teleprompter is going to make you sound trustworthy?

Note to all politicians: it does the exact opposite. You sound like a tight-ass, worn-out bag of utter bullshit. Bad!

Hillary ain't no saint, and Donald is no day at the beach. He was accused of groping eleven women, handily beating Bill Clinton's count of eight sexual misconduct allegations. Hillary made big money giving speeches to anyone willing to pay her exorbitant price; Donald bilked students out of hard-earned cash with a fraudulent university. She scrubbed cell phones to hide her sins; he refuses to release the tax forms that contain some of his.

But Trump's not a racist: the only color he sees is green. And Hillary's not a socialist: she's spent the last thirty years sucking money out of every available marketplace. In the end they're both just rich old white people trying to grab as much cash as they can.

More full disclosure: I voted for Hillary. But I sure as hell didn't want to.

She has more baggage than the day before Thanksgiving at LaGuardia Airport. Bernie Sanders seemed like a nice guy. Who should be running a Brooklyn arts commune. I dug Larry

David's Bernie Sanders on *SNL* more than Bernie's Bernie Sanders—mostly because Larry looked like he could make it through the first term without using an oxygen tank.

I chose Hillary because I don't believe geriatrically religious white dudes should tell women what they can or can't do with their bodies. Or that anyone should tell gay people who they can't marry.

Or a person who might have balls AND breasts where they can take a piss. What's the most important word in the phrase "transgender American soldier"? The middle one.

If there had been a great woman running on the other side—say Ana Navarro or Susan Collins—I would have gladly ticked a Republican box. And I wasn't alone. Tons of us felt like we had to choose between the lesser of two evils.

After it was all over, the mainstream media Monday morning quarterbacks talked about how the brash alt-right movement and economically stricken working class proudly brought The Donald into office. But I think part of the reason it came as such a surprise was because of all the "leaners" out there—folks who wouldn't declare it out loud the day before the election, but might sidle up to a friend the day after and sheepishly admit, "I voted for Trump."

Quite a few of my friends did that.

What state is our country in when we end up reluctantly casting our votes for politicians we don't believe in?

And if you think Trump's not a politician, try to find one time before this election cycle when he ever mentioned the word "Bible." Or "God." Or "faith." Search your memory bank. And the Internet. Both will come up empty. The closest he ever came to Christ was a Dominican busboy at Mar-a-Lago named Jesus. Not to mention all of the issues he changed colors on over the past five years—from abortion to the war in Iraq, to tax law, and yes, even Hillary.

And if she had won the race, the same public protests and ridiculous D.C. rabble-rousing we've seen for the last twelve months would be taking place in reverse. Instead of the Million Women March with pussycat hats, it would've been the Swollen Prostates on Parade with free Avodart and lots of extra porta-potties.

It's just flip sides of the same ancient political coin. The issues separating them and us can all be negotiated.

You wanna put a Democratic dent in the Republican armor? Stop stamping your social media feet and start planning to find an electable leader. You want another term of fat-cat Trumpian tax cuts? Quit gloating and get ready for a candidate not named Clinton. Democrats are whining about Republican bellyaching while absolutely nothing gets achieved—and our allies try to pull America's head out of its own ample ass.

Put the pettiness aside and let the negotiations begin.

Like Tom Hagen said: "This is business, Sonny. Not personal."

An approach Ronald Reagan and Tip O'Neill were savvy enough to take back in the 1980s. Tip was the Democratic Speaker of the House and not afraid to criticize the Republican president. Reagan did the same on a daily basis to his Democratic rival.

Until six o'clock in the evening.

Then they'd sit down for a beer or call each other on the phone and figure out what the most important piece of work was for each side that week—and they'd find enough common ground to pass legislation that made both parties happy.

After eight years of Obama fighting Republicans, and twelve months of Trump lashing out at Democrats and Republicans alike, it's time to act like Tip and Ron. Otherwise, we are screwed.

Two and a half centuries into being the Land of the Free and the Home of the Brave, where every citizen has the right to express his or her individual beliefs—a land full of complicated and multicultural tastes and opportunities—we've been broken down into two simplistic opposing teams: Left Wing Snowflakes versus Right Wing Nutjobs.

Libertards versus Conservadicks.

The Clinton News Network versus Fox's Fair and Balanced Republican Report.

Every single day it's another circadian dose of dogmatic talking heads caterwauling over each other on CNN and Fox until they get off the air to trade witless factional barbs back and forth during twenty-four-hour Twitter feuds. Sometimes I watch these paid reps from each party yelling into the void and I'm driven to stand inches away from the TV shouting back like a madman while I wave two ferocious middle fingers in their vein-popping faces.

We're living in an endless echo chamber where everybody's so busy bellowing across the divide they can't hear what the other side has to say. Doomed to forever repeat ourselves. Here's one solitary and true example I happened to stumble upon while watching TV:

On the morning of February 22, 2017, White House Press Secretary Sean Spicer stood at his podium and claimed the Democrats were manufacturing resistance by training and dispatching protesters to Republican town hall meetings to disrupt conversations about Trump's new health care plan.

Fox News ran the press conference live and then gave quick commentary on what bad losers the liberals continue to be.

Within minutes, at 11:25 a.m. to be exact, CNN produced footage from August 4, 2009, showing White House Press Secretary Robert Gibbs standing at the same podium claiming Republican Tea Party members were manufacturing resistance by training and dispatching protesters to Democratic town hall meetings in order to disrupt conversations about Obama's new health care plan.

CNN had quick commentary on how ironic it all was.

Within a few more minutes, at 11:29 a.m. to be just as exact, Fox News ran the Spicer footage followed by the Gibbs footage followed by a comment on how ironic it all was.

I would have switched back to CNN to see if they'd accuse Fox of plagiarism but I couldn't because MY BRAIN SUDDENLY REFUSED TO GIVE A FUCK ANYMORE!

Jesus!

And I'm not referring to the one in charge of cleaning Donald's dishes.

Recently this headline jumped out at my face: GYM BANS CABLE NEWS CHANNELS, CITING SAFETY CONCERNS. The YMCA gym in Scranton, Pennsylvania, had to put a block on CNN, Fox News, MSNBC, and the Fox Business Channel because bipartisan cardio sessions were leading to partisan fistfights as Democratic NordicTrackers disagreed with Republican treadmill runners. Equipment was being thrown around while people tackled and argued. Total chaos erupted as they screamed and chased each other. At one point the police had to be called in.

First of all, this sounds like an amazing workout. You get a great calorie burn from the chasing, total focus from the arguing, plus heavy lifting combined with kickboxing moves in addition to straining your neck muscles while engaging your physical and emotional core. Let's call it Nine Minutes to Partisan Power Abs!

My only problem: I'd want to kick every ass in that gym. Why? Because I can't listen to another pile of steaming Republican horse dung while ducking a flock of batshit Democrats anymore.

A lifelong Republican friend of mine was clenching his angry jaw recently as he recalled a workplace conversation with a Hillary supporter, who was still drenching social media with daily fanatical facts about the election ten months after it was over. Russia this and white supremacy that. Blah blah Bannon and yada yada Flynn.

They screamed back and forth until it reached a boiling point. Which is when my buddy got tired of what started to sound like acrimonious personal accusations and stood up for himself: "Finally I had to tell this asshole: 'Hey pal, I got nothin' against you people—some of my best friends are Democrats.'"

My heart sank. Have we really reached the point where an old-white-guy civil rights defense from 1962 is being recycled to explain our political situation in 2017?

Sad.

And I don't mean a Donald Trump overused, Twitter-type "Sad!" I mean truly, madly, deeply sad. As in distressingly so. Two Americans who no longer look at each other as fellow citizens, but as enemies from opposing armies: the Ruling Republicans versus the Dog with a Bone Democrats.

We've been reduced to and identified as being one or the other with no middle ground, very little wiggle room, and not one worthy alternative. Can you be a gun-toting, God-fearing, pro-life Democrat? Not unless you want your face chewed off by Nancy Pelosi. How about an atheistic, Meryl Streep–loving, Mexican-born Republican? Rudy Guiliani may eat your young. It's all a wall of electronic white noise with no nuance anymore. We're stuck in a self-righteous rut, endlessly bitching about Rachel Fucking Maddow or Sean Goddamn Hannity. With absolutely no gray area in between.

I'm here to say the opposite is true. This country is full of unpredictable people and wonderful contradictions. I'm here to tell you it's time for a new protest movement: Gray Lives Matter.

There's a ton of us out here who believe the extreme aspects of both parties are turning sane thinkers into cold outcasts as they lead us off the rails. All you have to do is open your Twitter app at any point in the day to witness a constant storm of blue impeachment tweets and red Republican retorts. As if the only thing social media can provide us is digital agita to incessantly reinforce our differences.

Even love isn't safe anymore. One in three Americans say that clashes over Trump have negatively impacted or ended their relationships. A flurry of so-called Trump Divorces have popped up in the court system, each involving implacable problems based on political affiliation. Which, to be fair, means they could also be called Hillary Divorces. Or Bernie Breakups.

This acrimony has reached all the way into the White House.

One Wednesday night last July, newly hired Communications Director Anthony Scaramucci famously told a reporter, "I'm not Steve Bannon—I'm not trying to suck my own cock." On Thursday morning Mrs. Scaramucci announced that she was filing for divorce based on her husband's "ruthless quest" to work for a president that she despises. By Monday afternoon, that president had fired her husband and the suddenly isolated and lonely Mooch was probably asking Bannon for some autofellatio lessons.

Once upon a time (because now it actually sounds like a fairy tale) Democratic Party strategist and Bill Clinton supporter James Carville was able to spend his days plotting to defeat President George HW Bush in the 1992 election before going home at night to sleep with Bush's campaign manager Mary Matalin. Who happens to still be his wife. And a Trump supporter. Along with one of their adult daughters. The other kid sided with her dad and voted for Hillary. They all still love each other and often have passionate political debates at the dinner table. Which always end with dessert. And hugs.

I still remember the days when almost everyone in America got along like the Carville-Matalin clan. Do you?

It was only sixteen years ago. Right after 9/11.

As the scent of acrid smoke, orange embers, and gray ash still clung to the cool September air above downtown Manhattan, Americans from all walks of life and each area of the country came in waves to help feed, support, and restore the spirits of New York City's cops and firefighters at Ground Zero.

Week after week, as these first responders dug through the twisted steel ruin and melted iron relics, seeking some sign of their fallen comrades, messengers of love poured into the Big Apple. I met people who had driven overnight from Cincinnati or all day long from Idaho, purely to put in volunteer time any way they could. The only smiles each morning were often due to lifelong New Yorkers meeting fellow Americans from Minnesota or New Mexico as they bonded over coffee before pitching in to help the city recover. At one point during the October efforts, a firefighter friend of mine said he felt as if he'd met someone from all fifty states, either while working the vaporous pile or taking a little time off to rest and recharge.

It was New York's Bravest and New York's Finest working hand-in-hand with America's Best. I was the lead guest on Letterman's second show after the attacks, and the live audience in the Ed Sullivan Theater was full of compassionate faces from every corner of the country. I'll never forget the tears in Dave's eyes during a break in the taping—so overcome with the shared emotion that was moving everyone in the studio and watching at home. During that awful autumn, New York's grief was felt in each town, hamlet, and metropolis across the nation. America truly felt like one united village.

Until Christmas was over.

In late January 2002, I fondly recall getting my first Manhattan middle finger in a long time—from a taxi driver who also loudly cursed me out as I was crossing Seventh Avenue against the light.

Four days after that, President George W. Bush swore revenge upon the Axis of Evil.

Four weeks after that: native New Yorker Tim Robbins was called a pussy by political pundits for opposing their upcoming Iraq war plans.

Four months later, policeman James Zadroga first suffered breathing problems related to his time at Ground Zero.

Four years further on and conservatives with presidential hopes were taking potshots at New York, calling it a nest full of liberal elites, as they geared up for the 2008 election.

And four years after all THAT, many Republicans—and a few Democrats—finally gave up their stubborn opposition to the Zadroga Act, which promised to compensate the families of first responders whose work at Ground Zero left them dead or dying.

Whatthefuck.com

It took less than one decade for us to go from a family of bipartisan patriots to a feuding bunch of asinine finger pointers. Eight years of George W. Bush ended with Republican infighting and Tea Party tears. Eight years of Obama finished with politically correct Democrats demanding apologies from edgier liberals who somehow invaded their safe space by expressing an opinion they are far too fragile to hear.

Both sides need to grow some balls.

We now live in an America so gluten-free that a box of jelly doughnuts is a bigger threat than Vladimir Fucking Putin. Where college kids are more afraid of Ann Coulter than HIV. Where you can tune every one of your digital devices into partisan shows that only say what you wish to hear and won't upset your statin levels. We're becoming political crybabies who climb inside sectarian Bubble Wrap and suck on our oh-so-sensitive thumbs.

I suck down jelly doughnuts two at a time with a Ted Cruz tome in one hand and an Al Gore atlas in the other—while making fun of each goddamn guy.

I'm taking a comic look at what's turned us into the Divided States of America, if for no other reason than to help us laugh our asses off about it. And in the true spirit of all our partisan pissing, this book will be an equal opportunity offender. Because ultimately we are all to blame for the problems that separate us. And very much together on what makes us NOT SUCK. Is a terror attack the only way we can all still come together? I believe we're better than that.

We're better than dueling partisan didactics harping their paid way through daily CNN shoutfests. We're better than Fox TV's *The Five,* where four Republicans maul a Democrat every night in a cloud of Trumpian agitprop. We should be able to rise above such grade-school-playground bully pulpit bullshit. We could use the digiverse to unify.

But we don't.

Last June, Rep. Steve Scalise and several others were shot by a crazed Bernie Sanders supporter during a 6:30 a.m. Republican baseball team practice session. Just after 9:00 a.m., commentators for both CNN and Fox expressed hope that all partisan politics could be put aside for a few days.

Those requests came about two hours too late.

Police had been called to the scene at 7:09 a.m. Dr. Laura sent out her first of fourteen tweets blaming Democrats at 8:05 a.m. This joined a river of Democratic tweets—blaming Republicans for the lack of gun control laws—that had begun rolling around 7:55 a.m. The president patiently stayed away from social media until he was able to visit the hospital that evening and get an update on Scalise's condition. After which he chimed in with a series of special tweets: one Pray for Steve, one Russia Witch Hunt, two Crooked Hillarys, and a Thank You, Wisconsin!

Ironically, we've all become so aware of his social media subject matter that his tweets start to sound like a list of baseball trading cards.

By the way, no matter who you voted for, don't fool yourself about our current party icons: they're all in the same business bed together. Hillary and Bill were VIP guests at Donald's wedding to Melania. Donald gave generous donations to Hillary's earlier campaigns and to the Clinton Foundation. Trump used to BE a Democrat, voting for and donating to many members of that party. Bill Clinton traveled the chummy charity circuit with George W.'s dad. And Trump defended his now notorious *Access Hollywood* pussy comments by claiming Bill said much worse things to him when they played golf together.

Which I pray to God we get to see again once Donald's out of office. What I wouldn't give to witness Bubba and a Tang-tone Trump playing eighteen holes with Billy Bush as their caddie:

TRUMP
How far would you say this putt is gonna break, Billy?

BILLY BUSH
About nine inches, sir.

TRUMP
So the same length as my dick?

BUBBA
Only if we're using the metric system. Hey, look at that blonde
over on the next tee.

BILLY BUSH
She's hot. I'd call HER a nine.

TRUMP
Great rack, average ass, lousy face. She's maybe a five in my
book. Would you fuck her, Bill?

BUBBA
Already did. Twice.

BILLY BUSH
You guys are SOOOO awesome!

Win or lose, they all make money just by being in the game. Hillary's latest book deal was for six million dollars. Barack Obama just signed one for forty million clams. And even though Donald only reads books he supposedly writes about himself, he'll pore over his next one for about a hundred grand per ghostwritten page.

While we're on the subject of books by ex-presidents, can we all agree not to build another useless, empty, and overpriced presidential library?

The latest estimates on Obama's planned tribute to himself hovers around a Holy Shit 1.5 Billion Dollars. Every single ex-prez feels the need to fund one of these monstrosities with architectural costs approaching a Martian space launch. And for what?

Most of them are located in some birthplace outpost called FuckKnowsWhere that maybe fifteen people visit on any given day.

We have finally chosen a nonreader to lead us—let's use his administration as the dawn of a new nonacademic, incurious, uninterested day. Because Donald's not alone. A recent study of the planet's most literate nations has America in twenty-third place.

Unless I read it wrong. USA! USA!

The fact that you are actually reading something that isn't a tweet, gossip item, or opioid prescription means you deserve a big pat on the back—and a better book than this. One written by a real author. With a page-turning plot, clever literary devices, and some deep emotional impact.

Sorry to tell ya but: you got the wrong Leary. My wife, Ann, writes those kinds of books. I can barely keep track of the keys to my truck, never mind a plot. Or a theme.

But I think we all expect more than that from the chosen few who serve as commander in chief—and then decide to write about it. We want insight and revealing historical, behind-the-scenes data with dollops of diamond sharp self-reflection. And what do they give us instead? Boring 800-page autobiographies full of blah blah me and yada yada you and glibbidy glob God Bless America. While the failed candidates they faced write vapid essay collections about Political Courage and Dreams That Refuse to Die.

Excuse me while I puke. Into a polling booth.

If Obama wrote an opus named *No I Couldn't,* my money would be plunked down on publication day.

I'd read a book by Donald Trump. If it was entitled *Trophy Wives and Tax Loopholes.*

But the only Hillary book I'll ever buy is one called *It Takes a Hammer: And Other Lessons in Destroying Digital Evidence.*

It's a literary given that the worse presidents perform in office, the more books they write after returning to private life. Jimmy Carter was a total disaster. He literally went on television at the height of the 1979 economic and energy crisis to blame all of us for causing his problems, telling us to stop being so selfish and capitalistic. We responded by showing him the exit sign and electing Ronald Reagan with a true, non-alternative-fact landslide of 489 electoral votes. Know how many books Carter's written since we chased him back to Georgia? Thirty. Including three in one year! And not one of them was called *What a Self-Righteous Asshole I Was.*

Nixon barely escaped a prison term after his presidency and instead wrote eight books. And then a ninth one came out AFTER HE DIED—like a bony hand in a B horror movie reaching out of the grave to say, "Damn right I was a crook—now pay me again, cocksuckers!"

By comparison, Ronald Reagan wrote one book. Bill Clinton wrote two. And George W. Bush wrote three—a book about his own presidential decision making, a biography of his father, and one very touching collection of paintings he made portraying members of the military injured in the line of duty after 9/11. With the proceeds going to help them recover. He's alone in that regard. And deserves credit for the effort.

Still, if you took the entire ex-prez literary oeuvre and collected it into just one of their bloated book museums, you'd be hard-pressed to fill up a single shelf. So what the hell are we building them for? Because they wanna see their names engraved on big chunks of steel and stone. And after they die their minions convince our government to pay further tribute with bridges and highways and airports.

Who the hell wants to tie their legacy to places and things we all end up swearing about? *Bumper-to-bumper on the LB* goddam *J. Stuck forever inside the Lincoln* fuckin' *Tunnel. Flight delayed again at JF* motherfucking *K.* You might as well lend your name to the Donald J. Trump Department of Motor Vehicles.

Ohhh—so tempting.

If these guys had any cojones, they'd pony up to the public for posterity: put your name on a free golf course, getaway spot, or subsidized open bar. Ask a New York City millennial what FDR stands for and they'll tell you it's the worst way to drive downtown. But if there was an FDR Pub with free booze from ten until closing time? Etch him into their minds for eternity. Most teens today discover the story behind Pearl Harbor after drinking one.

If Donald leaves office by announcing an annual worldwide Trump Hotel Free Spa Day instead of a library, even Hillary's grandkids will remember him fondly once a year. The Bill Clinton Massage Parlor, Carly Fiorina Facelift Center, Obama Basketball and Bong Dispensary, even a Ted Kennedy Duckboat Booze Cruise are guaranteed to make you immortal in the best possible way. If there was a Tip O'Neill Tequila we wouldn't have to explain who he was. People would still be toasting him with margaritas every single day, all around the world.

Some of you may say I'm debasing the Oval Office, but I'm just telling you how it really is: most Americans don't give a shit about pretentious books and sacred buildings. But free boob jobs and hand jobs? That's what democracy is all about.

The truth is that, by virtue of my success, I may now live among what is derisively called America's Out-of-Touch Elite, but I proudly rose up from its hardy Immigrant Working Class. I had a paper route when I was ten, and started washing dishes in a diner at age thirteen. All of my siblings and many of my cousins also worked there as waitresses, cooks, busboys, and cashiers.

I'm a first-generation Irish American. My parents came to this country by boat. My mom was a maid and my dad was a mechanic, carpenter, and electrician. Dad considered himself the luckiest man on the face of the earth because even though the closest he got to so-called wealth was painting rich people's houses, he was flush with friends and family—and his kids could go to college by virtue of scholarship money and government-supplied student loans. We were the first O'Learys and O'Sullivans to attend college on either side of the ocean. My mom still lives in the old neighborhood and is a constant lightning rod right back to my roots.

Even further full disclosure: I've worked on the sets of television shows with Donald Trump and he was not only on time and totally prepared, but charming and friendly with every single member of the cast and crew. He also graciously included the Leary Firefighters Foundation as a beneficiary during an episode of *The Apprentice*. I've hosted a charity event featuring Bill Clinton and had the pleasure of witnessing his ease and powerful abilities as a public speaker. I've met President Obama, been dazzled by his charisma, and sat in on one of his truly hilarious White House Correspondents' Dinner speeches. I've watched football with Chris Christie, memorialized fallen firefighters with Ted Kennedy, and stood side-by-side with Prince Charles to raise cash for one of his causes.

And I walked away from each and every one of these people even MORE impressed by my parents. So my take on today's

America really comes from their DNA: a healthy dose of humanity crossed with a dash of sarcastic common sense.

As a comedian, I'm looking forward to the next three years, with a possible four more tacked on—and not just because I want to play Kellyanne Conway in the President Trump biopic.

Which I do.

(Step aside, Jeffrey Tambor—I can already smell my Golden Globe.)

I think this country is at a crossroads and we need to make some changes. We are so entrenched in arguments over individual freedoms, so far apart on which future course we need to choose, and too deeply drawn to the empty fire that fame seems to provide. I'm an expert in that last area. And I have detailed opinions on the previous two.

Many of you may beg to differ with me. But you don't have a book deal.

So, for the next two hundred or so pages, this is all about what Dr. Denis Leary prescribes.

Ginger Rogers did everything Fred Astaire did. She just did it all backwards and in high heels.

—ANN RICHARDS, FORMER
GOVERNOR OF TEXAS

MADAM PRESIDENT

There will be one. Very, very soon.

Shattering the glass ceiling into smithereens.

She will come without previous baggage packed to cracking with cash earned through years of making Wall Street speeches for nine zillion dollars a pop.

Without a husband whose sexual track record reaches Caligula levels.

Without friends in high places who assure her of a victory so early in the race that she begins to hear only what she wants.

She will be funny and loose when the cameras roll, and not clinging to a teleprompter as if for dear life.

She won't be afraid to express her feminine side while also wielding a tough set of principles.

She will not need BleachBit.

She won't spend the first two hours of each day composing infantile tweets like a hormonal teenager.

She will also win without having to belittle her female opponents based on their physical appearance.

And in the heated battle of TV debates, her first instinct won't be to attack Megyn Kelly's menstrual cycle or tout the size of her own tits.

And she won't have to worry about fifteen men coming forward claiming she raped or molested them.

But her name will not be Elizabeth Warren or Liz Cheney. They are both successful and media savvy, but also lean too far left-wing moonbat and right-wing conservadouche to gather voters outside those realms.

Here are five women who could match Trump in business acumen and easily outwit him on any public stage: Mary Barra, Indra Nooyi, Marillyn Hewsom, Ginni Rometty, and Abigail Johnson—the respective heads of GM, PepsiCo, Lockheed Martin, IBM, and Fidelity Investments—who currently occupy the first five slots on *Fortune's* list of the Most Powerful Women in America.

I'm not telling you which political party they support. On purpose.

Because I don't care. Men have been seated in the ultimate position of power in this country for long enough. It's time to turn the reins over—time for a woman to tell us what we can or can't do with our prostates.

Can you imagine how hilarious it would be if our initial female president outlawed Viagra on her first day in office? Think it through. Then every man would know how it feels when women are told what they can or can't do with their vaginas by assholes who don't own one.

Our first female POTUS will also spend less time on her physical appearance each morning than our current president apparently does. Who do you want answering that emergency phone call at 3:00 a.m.—a woman who could jump out of bed and be ready to face the crisis in less than five minutes? Or a guy who needs at least another fifteen just to reconstruct and lacquer down his hair? Not to mention topping off the spray tan.

When it comes to being a drama queen, Trump's behavior veers into diva territory more often trod by Patti LuPone.

Official White House photographer Shealah Craighead has been ordered to carry around a stool while doing her job, so that she can photograph Trump from an elevated position, making him appear taller and slimmer. The last White House occupant to make that same request? Laura Bush. She started the trend by asking Shealah to shoot W. from above.

And while we're on the subject of looks, any woman would have more decorating sense than The Donald, whose taste runs toward Dictator Chic: giant slabs of new gold-flecked marble complemented by heavy gold drapes with gold braiding, hung inside rooms full of fake antique furniture with legs and arms edged in gold. It's a nouveau riche golden blizzard you'd expect to find in the home of a Third World monarch.

Or Elvis Presley. But I digress.

The real issue at hand is brains over brawn, touch over touché— cool instead of carried away.

Multiple scientific studies have all come to the same conclusions when comparing male and female performance based on genetic ability and statistical data. I'll spare you all the numbers and break it down into easy-to-understand terms. Here are the ten proven ways women are superior to men:

1. HIGHER IQ: Women are smarter. Like that's news.
2. PAIN TOLERANCE: Google "childbirth." End of argument.
3. MEMORY: My mom remembers everything I ever did wrong. So does my wife. And my daughter. So do yours.
4. DRIVING: Death by car crash happens to men 77% of the time. And you know who crashes into them? Not women.
5. NEGOTIATING: Women read body language and emotion with 87% more accuracy than men. Men don't know this. Why? Too busy reading Bleacher Report. And video game cheat sites.
6. SURVIVAL: Women live longer than men by an average of seven years, due to stronger immune systems and less risky behavior. (When I asked my ninety-year-old mom if we should pull the plug if she ever fell into a coma, she said, "I'll be pulling the plug on YOU if you don't quit smoking.")
7. INVESTING: The lack of testosterone leads to a much smarter and far less emotional approach to finance. Which would seem counterintuitive. Until you go to Vegas. Think back on the last time you saw a woman at a blackjack table full of drunken losers cursing their shitty luck and then inexplicably betting again. She was the dealer.
8. MULTITASKING: Women are capable of focusing on several things at once. Like making sandwiches for their children while having a detailed phone conversation about

work issues and simultaneously paying the gas bill via iPad. Men? You had us at "sandwiches."

9. EMPATHY: Women have an innate sense of compassion, caring, and kindness toward others. Men ask: Who are these "others"?

10. COMPUTER PROGRAMMING: Not even close. Probably because women spend their time online Googling technical breakthroughs instead of Eskimo porn. (Yeah, it exists. And yes, you can see their breath.)

If Trump screws up, the 2020 race could end with a woman in the Oval Office. If not, 2024 will be the next best option. And if Trump's proven anything with his ascendancy, it's that THIS announcement could happen at a State of the Union speech in the near future: "Mr. Speaker, the President of the United States—Ms. Oprah Winfrey!"

We're going to sell Jack like soap flakes.

—JFK'S FATHER, JOE KENNEDY, 1959

AMERICA'S GOT LEADERS!

Seven is a big number for humans.

Our skin cells regenerate every seven days. Our skeletal cells replace themselves every seven years. Most TV series that go past seven seasons are deemed to have jumped the shark. And most marriages end in divorce during year seven.

And within that Seven Year Itch is the Four Year Fall-Off.

Psychological studies of romantic relationships show that after four years "there is a vast dip in passion and satisfaction along with extreme boredom and seething anger."

Yikes.

Sixty-seven percent of couples report that the habits they found endearing at the beginning of the relationship became major turnoffs by year three.

It's kind of amazing, then, that our Founding Fathers so understood human nature that they had a hunch we should check our presidential love every four years. Some historians still claim that a limit of two terms was forced onto the presidency by Republicans angered by FDR's four-term legacy—which included victory over Nazi Germany, Japan, and the Great Depression. But it now stands as a sign of that Seven Year Itch invading our democracy: we fall in and then out of love. Sometimes in four years but definitely in seven.

However, these days that cycle has been shredded by our National Attention Deficit Disorder Syndrome (I'm calling it NADS). We hand a guy like Obama an economic crisis that would give FDR déjà vu, plus nineteen thousand other major issues we want solved, tell him to get to work, and within a few months stamp our feet, create the sarcastic #**ThanksObama**, and bitch about not having more cash to spend.

We point a flock of network camera trucks at Trump's White House the day he moves in and start cawing like tree crows as we criticize his failure to fix health care. It's impossible to stay infatuated with anyone after eighteen months of nonstop media exposure on the ever-expanding campaign trail. Elizabeth Warren and Cory Booker are already prepping runs for the 2020 Democratic nomination! Does it ever end? NADS or no NADS, we're overexposed.

Worry not, my friends. For I have a new cure for this particular political ill.

By the way, when Republican Twitter trolls drone on about how they don't want to hear what vain Hollywood celebrities have to say concerning politics, my response is this: too late, you just elected one.

It shouldn't be a surprise that in such a narcissistic, social-media-manic, selfie-obsessed society we chose to elect a reality

TV star to the highest office in the land. It makes perfect sense, given that the average American dedicates five hours a day to watching TV.

If we break that number five down it becomes even more troubling. Let's say we sleep (or try to) for eight hours, spend eight hours at work, and maybe two hours getting ready for and traveling to and from our jobs—that leaves us each about six hours of free time, five of which we spend parked on the couch.

Holy Diabetes, Batman.

And while there were an astounding 455 scripted TV shows to pick from last year, there were also an astonishing 750 reality shows on air. And 70% of us were glued to them for every single episode. It only stands to reason that after investing 1,918 minutes a week watching supposedly real people doing allegedly real things in purportedly real circumstances, reality TV would begin to convince our snack-addled brain cells that some of these morons might be smarter than us.

After all, they're on TV and you ain't.

Which is a terrifying but true side effect: we are buying into game-show-level bullshit. And trusting the host enough to think that at least one of them can hold public office and solve our country's issues the same way he solved TV problems on a Tuesday night. Donald Trump fires people on NBC, so let's send him to D.C. to get rid of every greedy fuckwad in this godforsaken government!

Let's face it, folks: as far as Trump's concerned, this IS a reality show. Video killed the radio star and now it's coming to eat our politicians. The famous are being swallowed up by the infamous. All bets are off on what qualifies someone to hold the highest office in America. You used to have to run an entire state or a city or become a senator to gain enough experience to aim for the Oval Office. Now you can just run some casinos into the ground, but as long as you used to have a hit show on TV . . . hey, put your left hand on the Bible and the other one in the air! It's time for at least four more seasons!

Just as NBC was firing him, The Donald's campaign began to take off and now he's the host of our ultimate reality TV show: *The Celebrity President*. A fact that left a lot of liberals condemning our democracy and fearing for our future.

But unlike them, I don't think this is the end of hope. As a matter of fact, Donald Trump's victory gave me a bracing blast of newfound faith in the system. 'Cause if his election proved anything it's that even I could be president one day. Look at his track record: angry tweets, canceled TV show, thin skin, and an attractive wife.

According to that formula, I'm one bad comb-over away from living in the White House.

Although, you don't want me running America. You think Trump takes too many trips to Mar-a-Lago? I'd be there the entire time. Sittin' in the sun, suckin' on buttered lobster legs, while my minions drop bombs on everybody. Starting with Yankee Stadium.

If we're gonna blur the lines between TV and reality, fuck it: let's make Kiefer Sutherland the next Democratic nominee. He seems to be able to handle a crisis pretty well on *Designated Survivor*. Plus he's also Jack Bauer, so he could personally kick some ISIS ass.

It might be time for a reality TV reality check.

Donald J. Trump isn't really a billionaire, but he played one on NBC. I played an FDNY firefighter on FX. Do you want me pulling up in a ladder truck when your house is on fire? No. All I'm going to do is curse the flames and light a cigarette off some smoldering debris.

Yeah, I know Donald's a billionaire on paper. But there's something fishy about the lack of published tax returns and the nine buildings in New York City that peeled his name off their edifices after the election. Turns out he doesn't actually own the buildings; he was just paid a licensing fee for the use of his name. Here's a little spoiler alert: actual billionaires don't have time to spend six months a year shooting a TV show.

You know who does? A celebrity with a brand to sell and products to move: Trump golf courses and hotel rooms. Trump vodka and shirts. Trump ties, meat, magazine, and airline. Not to mention the ultimate snake-oil salesman move: Trump University. Which was essentially a traveling circus that pitched its tent in various hotel ballrooms across the country to take your money in turn for supposedly teaching you how to get rich selling real estate.

Think about it. Why would a guy worth billions of dollars spend his valuable time hawking more products than Giuliana Rancic on an HSN Hydroxycut high? There's a reason you can't buy Warren Buffett Beef or Liliane Bettencourt Lingerie or a Paul Allen Guitar. Actual billionaires are busy all day, every day, taking care of business. Without going bankrupt.

Trump claims declaring bankruptcy four times proves how smart he is. You know what's even smarter? Getting box-shaped women to buy a zillion bottles of Skinnygirl booze and selling the company to Beam Suntory for a hundred and twenty million dollars. Does that make Bethenny Frankel a better business honcho than The Donald? When it comes to slingin' swag—fuck yeah. And the way we're going, maybe Madam Bethenny pouring Putin a Skinnygirl margarita in the Oval Office isn't such a pipe dream anymore.

But just like Giuliana, you gotta give Trump credit for embracing the power of TV. If a stick figure in designer denim can sell stretchy jeans to fat fucks, then surely an overfed orange man born with a silver foot in his mouth can sell himself as some kind of working-class hero to the actual working class.

No matter what you think about him, Trump was a master at communicating his message. He somehow captured the blue-collar imagination while sometimes hypocritically canceling out his own call to action. At his inauguration, a president who sells ties made in China ranted about other countries stealing American jobs to rabid supporters wearing MAKE AMERICA GREAT AGAIN hats manufactured in Vietnam.

You can't make this shit up.

If we had tried a scene like that in *Wag the Dog,* movie critics would have declared it waaay over the top. As they would this one: a rich guy who never swung a hammer in his life gets elected by convincing people who make, transport, and swing hammers for a living that he actually has something in common with them. Without even a posed photo op of him in work clothes at a construction site. Using any kind of hammer. Or standing near a hammer. Or even with his arm around Hank Aaron.

The only claim he made toward working-class credibility was when son Don Jr. talked about seeing his dad hang sheetrock at a work site one afternoon back in the eighties.

I'd say the closest that Don Sr. ever came to touching sheetrock was putting his fist through a wall in Trump Tower on the day he discovered his bald spot.

But he got the guys who DO hang sheetrock to believe in him. They saw Trump as a self-made man. Which is remarkable considering his white-collar background. During the election process he even admitted that it wasn't easy for him when he was starting out—he had to ask his father for "a small loan of a million dollars."

Sorry, Don, but that ain't a tiny advance. The day I graduated from Emerson College my dad gave me a card with a $100 bill in it. THAT'S what you call a small loan. And in my family, a hundred dollars was a lot of money. But you gotta hand it to him: Trump talked right to his audience. He promised them what they wanted to hear. He pushed all the proper buttons and got the desired response—much to many liberal chagrins.

So now we have a reality star in the White House and one of *TV Guide*'s 60 Nastiest TV Villains of All Time—Omarosa—as a trusted aide. She started out on *The Apprentice* before working her way up to other classy showcases, like alcohol-fueled bitch brawls on *Girls Behaving Badly* and slurping up slimy earthworms on *Fear Factor*. Now she works in the Oval Office sipping designer tea. So maybe it's time for us to rethink our election process, folks. Cut to the political chase. Update and eliminate. I'm using TV producer speak because I think that's what our current situation calls for: not less reality TV. More, more, more!

This is my proposal for future presidential contests: let's literally turn the election INTO a contest. The seemingly endless twenty-four long-winded debates of the past political year proved nothing except how low we could all go. So let's stop pretending we're operating on some imagined higher plane, step down into the gutter, and face the fact: it's all just one giant shit show.

And the shittier it gets, the higher the ratings.

Trump gets called out for groping eleven women and comes to the next debate surrounded by former Bill Clinton rape accusers and the ratings go through the roof. Nobody was paying attention to what Trump and Hillary said about the economy that night—we were all too busy waiting for a bad episode of *Empire* to break out.

Fuck the staid old-fashioned approach. We need something new. And we need it to be entertaining television.

Listen—we're Americans. We invented radio, TV, and the movies.

Well, an Italian guy named Marconi invented the radio, but we added commercials and made it profitable. And some strange cat named Eadweard (the word "weird" is right in his first name) Muybridge invented movies, but he only filmed horses running and people walking—we added the sex and guns and popcorn that made people really wanna watch. And some Scottish nut named Logie Baird invented TV, but we added the game shows, dick jokes, and titcoms that really made it worthwhile.

But we DEFINITELY invented reality TV, and we need to start using it to better effect. Right now all it shows us is self-centered, spoiled narcissists willing to fuck, fight, and backstab their way to the top of the pile. In other words: perfect presidential material.

No more political propaganda, no campaign commercials, no carefully controlled circumstances. Let's take *Survivor,* combine it with *So You Think You Can Dance,* add a dash of *American Idol,* and call it all *The Amazing New Presidential Race!*

Think of how exciting the 2016 election would have been if at the last second—live on international television—we got rid of the stiff, preplanned, over-sterilized debates. Imagine the political pandemonium when both sides were given on-camera challenges they were unable to ask Donna Brazile or Roger Ailes for help with in advance:

Could Hillary Clinton send a classified e-mail from her iPad to the White House without having an Anthony Weiner dick pic involved? Thirty-second time limit.

Would Donald Trump—armed only with a pack of Tic Tacs and Billy Bush—be able to spend fifteen minutes in a roomful of lingerie models without grabbing 'em by the pussy? Start the countdown.

Could Hillary and Senator What's His Face dance the samba? Make a pantsuit out of some palm fronds and chewing gum?

Could Mike Pence attend a Wednesday matinee of *Hamilton* and then get several cast members to Pray Away the Gay by the time the evening show began?

We shall never know, but it would have been RIVETING television. And unlike the debates, this format will inform us better about who the candidates really are. Actions speak louder than words. Crisis doesn't create character, it reveals it. Live on TV, if I have my way. In thirteen weekly episodes.

Fuck the conventions, the Super PACs, and the greedy trillionaire-lobbyist cabals. The entire run of this show will cost less than Melania's monthly shoe budget.

We stuff all the egos into a fancy house on August 14, start sending them out on time-driven missions with chaotic surprises on September 28, test their resolve with hidden cameras and sudden Hollywood-produced terror attacks on October 16—and in between we heap potentially embarrassing personal revelations on them, delivered by special guest ex-friends, lovers, and litigious enemies from their past. It's an edge-of-your-seat thriller full of angst, real-time reactions, and genuine faux pas.

I'd be a lot more enamored of Elizabeth Warren if she was running through the rain forest in a leather loincloth after stealing food from Sarah Palin's pup tent.

I wouldn't be able to blink while watching Cory Booker and Kirsten Gillibrand face a Democratic Dance-Off against Alec Baldwin and his yoga-toned wife.

There are so many delicious viewing options:

Mike Pence has to eat dinner—minus his wife—at a table full of liberal, attractive, pro-abortion women. Without getting sexually aroused or quoting the Bible. Then again, maybe reciting psalms is what gets him hot. Tune in and find out.

Bernie Sanders has to buy a new suit. And get it tailored. (This will take much longer than you think.)

Caitlyn Jenner explains designer vaginas to Rand Paul. With visual aids.

Kid Rock beats Kamala Harris in a playlist playoff with his new country rap remix of the national anthem.

Chris Christie wrestles with personal demons when a fresh

platter of Krispy Kremes is placed on the Brooklyn Bridge and the only way to save them is by blocking traffic in both directions.

Katy Perry tries not to fall asleep while Richard Dreyfuss discusses the making of *Jaws* and international diplomacy.

Tulsi Gabbard outsurfs Dwayne Johnson and live, bloodthirsty, non-Spielberg sharks.

Trump versus De Niro in a bamboo cage match.

Ted Danson versus Ted Nugent. Oprah Winfrey versus James Woods. Bruce Springsteen versus Bruce Willis: Battle of the Bruces!

It's all hosted by Dave Chappelle. With a panel of celebrity judges including Rush Limbaugh, Carrie Underwood, Mary J. Blige, and Howard Stern deciding who advances each week.

But come November 8, you vote for the ultimate winner while sitting on your sofa. With a cocktail in one hand and your iPhone in the other! What could be more American than that?

Admit it: the longer this chapter gets, the less crazy my idea seems. It's actually so simple I'm beginning to get chicken skin.

Let's be honest—the bright side of it all is NO MORE POLITICIANS. They'll be the first people voted off the island or not handed a rose or however it is we end up signifying losses. Because it's TV, celebrities will rule the roost. Which I consider progress. If Trump can run the country, why can't Halle Berry? I'd tune in to watch her press conferences, in full, any day of the week.

Which brings us back to square one: the audience. Listen—we really DON'T suck. Our better nature will win out. Like Winston Churchill once said: "You can always trust Americans to do the right thing—after they've tried everything else." Some of us are living in the modern world and some of us are stuck back in the days when Winston first said that, circa 1942.

We need to drag these people into 2018.

Probably the hard way.

Achievement has no color.

—ABRAHAM LINCOLN

JEW-S-A! JEW-S-A!

Racism is not only alive, it's very much thriving on social media and beyond. Because the one beautiful thing about racists is: they can't stop exercising their freedom of speech. Every ounce of idiot juice inside their ignorant little brains has to eventually be squeezed out and spoken aloud. Or tweeted. Or posted online.

Thank God.

Years ago I said something that's come to follow me around on the Internet in memes and various other media: "Racism isn't born, folks. It's taught. I have a two-year-old son. Know what he hates? Naps. End of list."

I'm no genius. I was just reflecting on the beauty of my young son's approach to life. He didn't care what color his friends were—he cared about what color their toys were. And how long they could all play with them before the much-dreaded afternoon nap invaded their imaginations.

I was a kid during the sixties, witnessing Martin Luther King's peaceful battle for civil rights on TV and made highly aware of

how to treat others based on a tool my immigrant parents educated us with: Judge everyone as an individual.

There was a great story on the news this year about a little white
kid whose best friend was black. Jax, the white kid, and Reddy,
his black friend, both decided to get the same haircut so their
kindergarten teacher wouldn't be able to tell them apart. It was
one of those moments that make you swoon over the innocence
and purity of children.

For my son's generation—as well as the one Jax and Reddy are
a part of—all men truly are created equal. Their actions reflect
friendship based on content of character, not skin color. They
have grown up with a black president in office for eight years.
Which was a major accomplishment for this country. Let's face
it—we've always been great. Complicated? Yes. Imperfect? You
bet your ass. But the thing that makes us great is our striving to
BECOME perfect. Always moving forward to try and solve our
problems and right our wrongs.

So when I heard the motto "Make America Great Again," my
first reaction was: *What the fuck is Trump talking about?*

It sounded like if he had a time machine, it would magically
transport us back to a period when things WERE perfect in
this country. But he's only ten years older than me, so when exactly would that be? In 1948 when he was two years old? The
early fifties, during the McCarthy hearings and the beginning
of the Cold War? Maybe it was the sixties, when assassinations,
race riots, and the generation gap tore the nation in half. Then
again, he could be referring to the herpes-free, pre-AIDS 1970s
"Me Decade" when disco ruled and you only had to wait in line
for seven hours to fill your car with gas. Or the trickle-down-
economics eighties, when the rich got richer and the poor got

crack. It's definitely not the nineties, when the country flour-ished financially, because no Republican wants to credit a Dem-ocrat who finally balanced the federal budget.

And thought it entitled him to free head.

I like to call this approach Americonomics—the belief that we can re-create some great aspect of the past if the right person is put in charge. But it's just another haul of horseshit: Trump's not bringing manufacturing jobs back, because Chinese facto-ries will always be cheaper. Coal miners can rejoice as Trump pulls back Obama's environmental rules, but their jobs are being stolen by machines that don't have lungs. Trump will tax cut this and deregulate that and make a big splash out of sign-ing the paperwork. It actually makes zero mathematical sense, but the pronouncements play well at arena rallies. He's basically becoming the head Cheeto of his own cheering masses: loud, puffed up, and full of orange air.

I've been living in America for almost six full decades and it al-ways gets better as we go along. If you gave me a time machine, I wouldn't go backward at all. I already did 1977. Sure, you could fuck whoever you wanted without a condom, but there was al-ways a shitty Bee Gees tune setting the mood. No thanks. I'd go forward, knowing this country would be even better no matter what year I picked.

Because America is an amoeba—ever changing, ever morphing, ever alive. With the food, music, and ideas brought to this coun-try from numerous other nations. Some of us may gaze upon the Statue of Liberty as an old iron lady. Like Hillary jokingly said, Donald Trump looks at her and sees a four, maybe a five if she loses the torch.

I still see Lady Liberty as my mom and dad first did when passing by her on a boat as they arrived in New York Harbor from Ireland back in the 1950s: full of promise and potential. Welcoming every color, creed, and creative impulse.

The problem with "Make America Great Again" was its resonance with a lot of people in this country who don't like progress. Or black people. Or Jews.

As I said earlier, the only color Trump can see is green—and whatever that shade of tanning cream is that he plasters on his puss. But his loud and brash campaign appearances and nostalgic motto caught the attention of some assholes who decided this was the perfect opportunity to tout their own out-of-date, throwback tendencies.

One of which was good old-fashioned American racism.

And let's be clear: we're not talking about questionable racism. Like calling someone who offered even the tiniest criticism of Obama's economic policies a racist. Or saying that if you boo a black shortstop after he strikes out for the third straight time, you're a racist. We're talking blatant, on-camera, 1963-style hatred and stupidity.

It's awful and ugly and unforgivable. But my approach is this: if you're gonna be a hater, by all means be honest and up front about it.

Don't be like the Arizona housepainter George Lindell who fervently and repeatedly chanted "JEW-S-A! JEW-S-A!" at the media pool during a Trump rally last year. In full view of a press bull pen jammed with cameras, George screamed and jabbed the air with his MAKE AMERICA GREAT AGAIN signs and HILLARY FOR PRISON T-shirt on proud display. After the videos went viral, George went back on camera the next day—beer and cigarette in hand—to claim he worked with a lot of Mexicans and liked the way they pronounced the *U* in USA as "Ju" and decided to pay tribute to them in public.

"I'm around Mexican people all the time," George explained. "I speak Spanish a lot. That's my lingo. It's just the way I say it. It had nothing to do with the Jews. You media people are so paranoid."

Nice try, Georgie.

Say what you want about David Duke, but he would never use Mexican housepainters to explain away an anti-Semitic Jewish-media rant.

He's too busy hating black people.

But karma's a bitch. Which is why David Duke's facelift makes it look like he's creating a master race of sixty-seven-year-old lesbians. The Arizona rally video actually shows George pointing at reporters and camera operators, shouting, "You're going down, you're the enemy! You're the ones working for the devil! We're run by the Jews, okay? Yeah!!!"

And the spin he put on his story turned into a hanging curve-ball, because the so-called Jewish media hit a home run when they found his Facebook page. Upon which—around the same time—he posted: "War with Russia? Sounds like a good time to shoot amerikan democrats in the back or face!" Under the name of his company, Lindell Paints, on the Alex Jones website Infowars.com, there were several uses of the word "nigger" and harsh talk like this: "It is not murder when you kill a nigger, it is animal abuse, which is sometimes needed, just look at your own dog." He at first denied writing the comments, saying they were composed by his "helpers," but then said he supported them one way or another before taking down the business page and erasing his Facebook presence.

Here's a headline you probably saw coming: George denies that he's a racist. Or that he hates Jews and black people. In his final appearance in front of the cameras he said, "The human race is just one race, dumb-ass. 'Niggers' is a word in the English language. Do you know how popular that word was in 1902?"

I guess we know which year George would travel back to if he ever got his hands on that time machine.

George also said he lives near a lot of black people, with whom he gets along fine. Not to mention Jews: "I happen to fucking love the Jews. Most of my customers are Jews!"

Not anymore they ain't.

It's gotta blow to carry that much hate and deception around in your heart every day. As a Boston sports fan I hate the New York Yankees, the Montreal Canadiens, and the Los Angeles Lakers. But it's not based on the color of their skin. It's the color of their uniforms. And during the playoffs I can get overheated about it.

But a guy like George? He's gotta feel that heat times ten thousand every single waking moment of every single day. To paraphrase an old saying: it's not the hate that gets you, it's the fake humility.

George's Trump-rally rants reflect the old-school racist belief that the media is run by big-brained Jewish billionaires with an ax to grind. Let's examine that idea for a second:

- The major shareholder of *The New York Times* is a Mexican zillionaire named Carlos Slim Helú. He is a Maronite Catholic Christian.

- Television and media giant Liberty Media is owned by Irish American John Malone.
- Warren Buffett is an agnostic.
- Rupert Murdoch's father was a Presbyterian, and he has often dabbled with the idea of becoming a Catholic.

I could go on and on, but why bother.

Let's instead focus on the rabid chanting of "U-S-A! U-S-A!" that so inspired George's Jew-baiting reinterpretation and was the rolling-thunder cry at all of Trump's campaign rallies. It arose from the desire for America to be number one again. In fact, we are number one in quite a few areas. Experts have done the math and the stats don't lie, ladies and gentlemen:

Mass shootings? We are not only number one, but so far ahead of numbers two through ten that even COMBINED they can't compete with us.

And guns? Not even close. We've been number one in manufacturing them for decades, and we're only making MORE guns. And bullets. And bombs. We have more guns than anyone else on earth. Serbia comes in second, but almost forty percentage points behind. Yemen is third, and seventy-two points back. Suck on our spent shell casings, bitches!

And you'll never guess what else we lead the world in:

Nothing. That's right. Zip. Zilch. Nada.

According to a vast study of world power and performance called Best Countries Rankings—compiled annually by the consulting firm Young & Rubicam's BAV LAB and the Wharton business school—we ain't what we used to be.

Wharton is, of course, our current president's alma mater—the school so often mentioned whenever Trump talks about how smart he is. So I think we can trust their findings in what might as well be called the Actual Olympics. Sure, we win a ton of gold medals when we run track, ski, swim, and skate. But in real life, we can barely win a bronze.

In Overall Performance we come in seventh place. Which may sound bad but means we at least make the playoffs.

In Best Country for Women we place sixteenth—just squeaking into the postseason.

Inclusiveness: seventeenth—still in the Wild Card race.

Quality of Life, we barely beat Portugal for eighteenth and early golf.

Best Country for Kids, we are nineteenth—with no participation trophies.

Attracting Investment from Other Countries, we finish thirty-fifth. Behind fucking Uruguay. And have to pay for the rebuilding year ourselves.

Health Care: fiftieth. That's not a typo: we finish fiftieth. Don't Google numbers one through forty-nine. It will only make you sick. Which could literally cost you an arm and a leg under TrobamaCare. Plus your house.

There are some bright spots. Entrepreneurship: we take the

bronze behind Germany and Japan. Cultural Influence: we also get bronze after Italy and France.

In Racism we nab the number five spot. Which is better than finishing first. Unless you're George or David. Then you're pissed off.

More good news! In the category of Worst Airports in the World we place silver (Newark), bronze (LaGuardia), and fourth place too (JFK)!

And in the Highest Rate of Diabetes category we get the gold! Just barely beating out Malta and Singapore. Whew, that one WAS close. But on an annual basis, ice cream kills more Americans than ISIS ever has. Forget the terror attacks, just send us a free supply of Chubby Hubby. Ten years from now? BOOM! Diabetes Bomb.

And here's some more good news: in Drug Abuse and Dependency we finish eighth overall, but in Prescription Drug Abuse we grab the gold for Biggest Opioid Addiction.

O-S-A! O-S-A!

Let's hear George chant THAT.

With the exception of KKK members and other dedicated public white supremacists, your average everyday racist never really believes he or she is one. They couch it in politically correct terminology or fold it into sociological concerns. Then again, how many times has a moron walked up to you and said, "Sorry, I'm a total fucking moron" after acting like one? And how many times have you seen a douchebag raise his hand and say, "Hey, everyone! I'm a giant douche!"

Answer: Not once. Ever.

George may think because he works with Mexicans and adopted their language it makes him a mensch. It doesn't. It makes him a racist in two different languages. Let's go deeper on the JEW-S-A! idea. Studies show that only seven million Jewish people live in the United States, and that two and a half million of those live in the New York/New Jersey area.

JEW-S-A?

Sorry, Georgie, but based on the numbers? That antique fanaticism ain't ever gonna fly.

But JEW YORK, JEW YORK, is a distinct possibility and has always been a celebrated sobriquet for the Big Apple. The many contributions of its Jewish citizens are one reason why New York has always led the world in offering up true comic genius and elegantly intelligent ideas.

Like not being a bigot.

As for the rabid anti-immigrant and Pure White Pride approach to current life in this country, that's a despotic dream that guys like George need to let go of.

'Cause it's already dead.

Here's the most recent chart explaining the twenty-first-century makeup of the American populace:

2010 FEDERAL POPULATION ANCESTRY CENSUS
  1. GERMAN   50 million
  2. AFRICAN   45 million

3.	IRISH	35 million
4.	MEXICAN	32 million
5.	ENGLISH	27 million
6.	AMERICAN	20 million
7.	ITALIAN	17 million
8.	POLISH	10 million
9.	FRENCH	9 million
10.	SCOTTISH	6 million
	Tied:	
11.	SCOTCH-IRISH	5 million
11.	NATIVE/ALASKAN	5 million

That's right, George—Germans apparently rule the roost in America by five million people.

GERMAN-S-A! GERMAN-S-A!

Meh. Doesn't sound that great. Matter of fact, it sounds vaguely like one of Hitler's secret military branches. For which George and his ilk might actually march in a parade. Oy.

You know what sounds better? A-S-A! The African States of America. They finished in a very close second place. But the truth is, there are probably twenty million illegal Mexicans running around, so if you add them in with their registered American citizen ancestors, we're talking first place with over fifty million total.

U-S-M! U-S-M!

It actually has a nice ring to it. And by the time of the 2020 census may technically be true. Plus, George knows the language already so he should make out fine in the United States of Mexico. He could teach them all about 1902.

The group I'm most curious about is the one at number six: Americans. Nobody is really just American; we all originally came from somewhere else. Only one of the groups tied for eleventh place—Native and Alaskan Americans—can claim ownership to this land before the rest of us rolled in on boats waving European weapons and planting empire flags.

But twenty million of us chose to do what my dad did back in chapter one—drop all the other qualifiers and label themselves with a single word. Which reflects their pride about having either moved here themselves or being the progeny of someone who did. Conquering oceans and mountains. Deserts and despotic regimes. Economic distress, repressive governments, murderous movements, and any number of other odds. No matter the obstacle, freedom remains a powerful beacon. For decades, many Cubans made the 103-mile trip to Florida after spending seven days in the searing sun on rafts made out of items like patched-up old inner tubes. Surrounded by the most shark-infested waters on the planet. Eating nuts and berries.

And you think a wall is going to keep these people out? Or a travel ban?

Not unless you can also ban ladders and tunnel digging. Along with pole vaulting and catapults.

Plus ingenuity.

Not to mention the human spirit.

This isolationist attitude, undercut with a vaguely xenophobic hope that somehow cement can keep crime and drugs at bay, is a modern-day unicorn. Full of reductive delight. Drug lords are in a zillion-dollar supply and demand business. As long as their best customers live here, they will find another way in. Criminals go where the cash flow leads them. When someone famously asked Willie Sutton why he kept robbing banks, his answer was: "'Cause that's where they keep the money."

I like immigration. It's how my parents came here. Plus, I'm not ready to give up any of the good ideas immigrants introduce to America. 'Cause their track record on that over the years is pretty fucking impressive:

Cannolis, tacos, knishes, croissants, pasta. Egg rolls, French fries, pierogi, pizza, sausage, bratwurst, sushi. Muffins, beer, scotch, tequila, vodka, whiskey, lager. Jazz, blues, rock, hip-hop, and every show tune ever written. Cars, planes, trucks, trains, TV, radio, film, laptops, iPhones, and photography.

Life would suck without this stuff. Once again, I'm not interested in reversing time. Because there have always been those who firmly believe they should be the last new people allowed to enter this land. Going right back to the original settlers, who fought like hell to keep other explorers out. Think about that. If we had stopped immigration right after the Pilgrims landed, we'd still be eating maize and buffalo jerky three times a day. And telling long stories around the campfire at night. Pass me the fucking firewater, Chief.

But Trump's still adamant about his wall solving Mexican immigration, our drug problems, and crime. So let's examine this monstrosity.

First off, it's been described as a wall—but even Trump has admitted that some of it may need to be a fence. Other Republicans have described it as a wall with sections that would be a "wall-like fence." Still others have termed parts of it "a fence-like wall." So how much is this fency wall or wallish fence or fwall or wence actually going to cost?

Well, we're talking 1,954 miles. Minus 652 miles that already have barriers. Those barriers consist of wallfs and fwences that cost 2.3 billion dollars to build fifteen years ago. So we're left with roughly 1,300 miles that need coverage.

In June 2016, Trump estimated that his fifty-foot-high concrete wall would cost 8 billion dollars and take two years to build. In July, the Bernstein Research Group studied the situation in-depth, concluding it would cost between 15 and 25 billion and take seven years to erect. Trump must have thought that was fake news because in October he updated his estimate to 12 billion dollars and two and a half years. By February he was claiming a 15-billion-dollar price tag and three and a half years.

We haven't even broken ground yet and already this thing has almost doubled in price and time.

Several construction experts from the states involved expressed concern about the situation due to their experience with local permits and personnel expenses. Trump's team forged ahead, confident in their aims and buoyed by the energetic response of their supporters for what a bold leader is capable of doing with a patriotic focus and a fistful of power.

Let's review one example of what happens when the federal government decides to work with state and city officials to pull off such a monumental task: The Central Artery/Tunnel Project in Boston, Massachusetts.

Its unofficial title was the Big Dig—and it involved tearing down the ancient expressway in downtown Boston, replacing it with an underground tunnel system and, above it, a cityscape of grass and parkland crisscrossed with updated city streets. It was one of the last deals worked out between Ronald Reagan and Tip O'Neill, joining federal money and altruism with state necessities and local expertise to prove they could all solve one of America's growing issues: failing infrastructure.

It would ultimately combine a tunnel named after the iconic baseball and military hero Ted Williams with one named for Tip O'Neill himself, plus a greenway dedicated to former first mom Rose Kennedy. It would be the biggest and most expensive federal road construction project in the history of the United States, scheduled to take seven years at a cost of 2.8 billion dollars.

And guess what? They did it.

They built the modern equivalent of the Roman aqueducts and not only did it reduce traffic, it made the downtown area a beautiful and much more accessible place. It made international news and attracted unlimited media attention. It made Boston synonymous with federal solutions for state and city issues.

And it only took seventeen years and 22 billion dollars.

You read that right: ten years longer than estimated, at almost ten times the cost. The project was plagued from day one by design flaws, poor execution, escalating prices, schedule overruns, unexplained delays, substandard materials, and massive corruption. In other words: it was just like everything else Washington decides to do.

And it only covers 3.5 miles of land.

You also read that right: it's only three and a half miles long. And we used Mexicans to help build it.

Three and a half miles is 0.26923076923077 percent of 1,300 miles.

I'm no math genius, folks (I Googled the percentage), but how long do you think it will really take our government to build a cement structure that runs from California to Texas, after they spent almost two decades building one that runs from downtown Boston to downtown fucking Boston?

Here's my answer: forever.

And by "forever" I mean at least fifteen years and 50 billion dollars. Or 940,203,083,866 pesos. Which is what Mexico will supposedly pay us for our efforts.

By the time it's done, Trump's youngest son, Barron, will be old enough to run for office. And collect our cash from south of his daddy's wallyfence albatross. Congressman Barron Trump will be in charge of a 20% tariff his father wants to place on all Mexican imports to the USA. Let's take a look at what that includes:

Mexico provides us with 93% of our avocados, 71% of our tomatoes, and 1.3 billion dollars' worth of our beer. Plus 80% of our tequila. And about half of our Coca-Cola. Not to mention a ton of our snacks.

I know—we could easily give all that up, right? And these:

Most of our truck and automobile tires. And engine parts. And vehicle parts. As well as whole vehicles from Nissan, Honda, and Volkswagen. As well as all Cadillac Escalades, Chevy Silverados, Dodge Ram trucks, and Ford Fusion cars.

Plus every G5, Gulfstream, and Lear jet. And most of our plasma TVs.

Also a shitload of important computer and cell phone parts—the final pieces before the devices are delivered to market. And medical instruments. And refrigerators. As well as most of our air-conditioning units and Fender Stratocaster guitars, 70% of all our vegetables, and 41% of our fruit. And irony of all ironies . . . most of our cement supply. Which we need to build the wall.

Wow.

So, just to put it in perspective, we will actually be paying higher prices for almost everything we eat, drive, watch, and talk into on a daily basis, including the main ingredient we need to build the wall that is aimed at protecting us. This may go down as the single most idiotic idea in immigration history. We're going to make Mexico raise the prices on products we buy from them to pay for a wall we already used our money and their cement to build?

Call me crazy, but it sounds like we're getting fucked. Twice.

Maybe even three times.

Why don't we just build the wall out of pickup trucks and Stratocasters? Throw in the odd refrigerator every couple of miles so you can grab a cold Corona on either side.

The mayor of Brownsville, Texas—the town where the wall would end—is Democrat Tony Martinez. His take on the project: "Nearly impossible." Republican representative Will Hurd, whose district includes 800 miles of the Texas border, says, "It WILL be impossible and also the most expensive and least effective way to secure the border." I could quote more local opinions from experts in the terrain bordering Mexico—including deserts, wetlands, mountains, rivers, grasslands, and forests—but you get the point: it's the Ted Williams Tunnel times twenty-fucking-five. With bipartisan critics who live along the line.

Hey, if Trump really wants to fund a foolish notion with our money, why not use one of his signature phrases and "go bigly"?

Fuck the wall. Let's build a bubble.

A giant bulletproof plexiglass bubble that bombs and bad weather can't penetrate. Just like the bubbles on top of arcade table-hockey games, it would cover the entire country. No one gets in, nobody gets out. Studies show that most Americans have very little interest in foreign vacations anymore, and the ones that still do can watch the Travel Channel.

The Bad Hombre Bubble Project (my title) will take two years from start to finish. And only cost us ten billion dollars. How do I know that? Because I just made it up. Which is essentially what most politicians do. But people are gonna love my BHB hats and buttons. And if Trump's wall isn't built by 2020, I could run against him wearing both and probably win by touting my "big, beautiful, see-through bubble."

Think of the possibilities: plenty of sun but no rain or snow. No future 9/11-type attacks! And no more pesky tourists!

B-H-B! B-H-B!

I bet we lead the world in stupid chanting. Which would suck. But nobody's ever measured that particular statistic, so there isn't any proof. Thank God. But let me remind everyone about something great that America has ALWAYS been the undisputed champion of: charity. Giving time and money to help others. Donating hard cash and tender caring. Literally our blood, sweat, and tears. This is an area in which nobody can compete with us.

Shit.

I just Googled "Top Ten Most Charitable Countries" and we're officially not number one anymore. Myanmar is—a place that sounds like it's named after marshmallow-filled candy. But that's okay, because we're still the number one most positive place on the planet.

Fuck.

I just Googled "Ten Most Positive Countries" and we come in ninth. Jesus. Behind Singapore and Germany. What the hell? This is really bumming me out. Listen—it's not a problem. Because I'm positive we are still the most positive place in the Western Hemisphere.

Goddammit.

Just Googled that. It's Canada. Probably because there's more alcohol in their beer. Okay, so we're the second most positive place in the Western Hemisphere. That's fine.

Motherfucker.

You're not going to believe this: it's Cuba. They're all happy as hell 'cause Castro finally kicked the bucket. Still not a problem. Here's what we're going to do:

There are only 54 million people in Mallowmar and barely 11 million in Cuba, so I'm declaring victory based purely on population. I mean, I've got at least 10 million Irish American cousins and they all become extremely happy big tippers after a few Jamesons. So let's call it all a draw. As of right now, Dr. Denis Leary says we ARE the most positive and charitable people on this big, blue and white marble.

We don't want to pay for your health care, yet if your house gets crushed in an earthquake, we will pull you out and hand you a sandwich. It might be a Big Mac, but hey, you were just trapped under a house. I don't think this is the time to start counting calories.

Great things happen every day in this country. Many of them are achieved by people standing on the shoulders of their parents, grandparents, and the Founding Fathers. Meanwhile, every day more new faces arrive: poor, tired masses yearning to breathe free and stake their claim to the American Dream. A wall won't keep them out. A bubble won't hold them in. To paraphrase *Field of Dreams*: if you build it, they will still come— under it or over it. Or even right through it. You can't legislate courage away from a heart. You can't outlaw desire deep in a soul. But when you welcome both, brilliance is born.

The Americans in the next chapter are examples of what happens when dreams meet reality. And what will always keep us number one in the category of Most Sought-After Place to Live.

A people that values its privileges above its principles soon loses both.

—PRESIDENT DWIGHT D. EISENHOWER

RED, WHITE, AND TRUE

It has been my pleasure in this life to meet many people who have become inspirational figures for me. People who make this country not suck, every single day. I've written a lot about my parents in the past, and even in these pages. There isn't a day that goes by without something they taught me through their words or actions coming back to help illuminate the present. My wife, Ann, is a daily beacon of light who makes me laugh and solves any problem, big or small, with common sense and a clear moral compass.

But there are other friends and family members who not only make my life better for being in it, but make America better by virtue of how they live theirs. A few of them are famous. The rest of them should be.

For all the right reasons.

* * *

One day in 1991, Michael J. Fox was still riding the high of a huge Hollywood acting career. Gifted with the rare combination of good looks and astonishing comic timing, he had won well-deserved Emmys for his role as Alex Keaton on the smash sitcom *Family Ties,* and his *Back to the Future* film trilogy had manufactured billions of box-office dollars while making audiences all over the planet laugh out loud.

He noticed a twitch in one of his pinkie fingers. And wrote it off as the result of some stunt work gone wrong. Mike was also a good athlete, Canadian born and raised with a hockey stick in his hands and skates on both feet. Fast, nimble, and built low to the ground, his secret weapon on and off the ice had always been people who underestimated his ability based on physical size.

That all changed when doctors diagnosed that pinkie twitch as the first sign of Parkinson's disease.

Mike responded to the news the way I would have: by drinking himself into oblivion. How was it possible that such a successful, smart, funny, and physically capable guy could get hit with news like that at age twenty-nine?

The answer: Parkinson's doesn't discriminate.

His wife, Tracy Pollan, focused his energy back onto their young family and soon Mike had not only sought help to quit drinking, but learned as much as he could about the other disease his body was now burdened by. Adopting the motto "You don't die from Parkinson's, you die WITH it," he formed the Michael J. Fox Foundation and dedicated himself to finding a cure. Since 2000, the foundation has become the largest nonprofit funder of Parkinson's research in the world, investing more than 650 million dollars so far.

And to think that all of this started with a speedy little skater from Vancouver who happens to be one of the funniest motherfuckers I've ever known.

Once Mike and I were on vacation together and headed to the gym. We hadn't seen each other in a while, and I noticed he was still in really great shape.

"Whaddaya doing for cardio these days?" I asked.

Mike replied, "I'm doing a lot of shaking. It's called the Parkinson's Workout."

It took me a few minutes to catch my breath as I stood on the beach laughing my ass off.

That's the thing about Mike that never ceases to amaze me. His sense of timing is impeccable, but his ability to accept bad circumstances and adapt them into positive results is truly remarkable. And he turned that point of view into several best-selling books, sharing his hopeful approach with the rest of the world—most notably in his acclaimed memoir *Always Looking Up,* the writing of which took its toll. As with any book and any author, Mike found himself mired in a bout of writer's block and grunting angrily around the apartment until Tracy asked him what was wrong. He answered in this fashion:

"I'm never gonna finish my book about fucking optimism!"

It was Tracy's laughter at that self-pity that finally turned him around. He finished the book. He went on to win more Emmys after starring on *Rescue Me* and *The Good Wife*. He continues to conquer Parkinson's one day at a time. And to be one of my favorite people who ever walked this earth. Because of all the titles attached to his world-famous name—Actor, Producer, Author, and Activist—the most important one to him is Dad.

* * *

During his Hall of Fame National Hockey League career, Cam Neely virtually invented the position now known as the power forward. He was six foot two and 220 pounds of pure muscle. Traded from his hometown Vancouver Canucks to the Boston Bruins in 1986, Cam flourished as a first-line right wing. Hockey fans in Boston and around the world fell in love with his ferocious, full-speed, all-heart style of play.

Multiple All-Star Team selections pointed to a razor scoring touch coupled with the devastating body checks that made Cam's presence on the ice a scary problem for opponents to cope with. He once scored fifty goals in only forty-four games, a feat surpassed only by Wayne Gretzky. He could shoot, score, and kill you in the corners.

But while being lauded in the sports world and considered a hockey icon, off the ice Cam was dealing with an enemy he never saw coming.

In 1987 his mother, Marlene, was diagnosed with colon cancer, to which she ultimately succumbed at the young age of forty-seven. Just a few years later, his father, Michael, was diagnosed with a brain tumor and passed away in 1993 at age fifty-six. Suddenly Cam found all his wealth, talent, and fame useless against a disease that was ravaging his family.

In 1994, he decided to do something about it and started the Cam Neely Foundation for Cancer Care. The first goal was to gather enough money to build the Neely House at Tufts Medical Center in downtown Boston, a special wing of that hospital devoted to helping patients and their families have the ultimate comfort and care while being tended to by many of the world's finest cancer specialists. By 1997, the Neely House was up and running. By the year 2000, it had expanded to over 16,000 square feet.

In the twenty-two years since its inception, the foundation has moved even further into finding and financing a cure. Other avenues that Cam's work has opened include the Neely Center for Clinical Cancer Research, the Neely Cell Therapy and Collection Center, the Neely Pediatric Bone Marrow Transplant Unit, the Michael Neely Center for Brain Tumor Care and Research, and the Marlene Neely Endoscopy Suite. All of these spaces—and the amazing work being done in them—are dedicated to the memory of his parents.

The Neely House has lovingly housed over seven thousand families during the last two decades, to make life easier as they battle the disease. It even touched the comedy community when Jimmy Fallon's father was successfully treated there. The research side of the foundation continues to make breakthroughs and expand.

Inducted into the Hockey Hall of Fame in 2005, Cam is a unanimous first-ballot inductee into the Humanity Hall of Fame, whenever they decide to open one. He brought the grit, grace, power, and multi-tool ability of his hockey career to the battle against cancer, and it's never stopped paying off.

I've played hockey with and against Cam and let me tell you something: WITH is way better. His competitive drive and fierce desire to win overcome every obstacle when he is on the ice. The wrist shot that made him Patrick Roy's least favorite attacker is deadly accurate. The body size that made him such a hurricane on skates fills you with fear. And the look in his eyes when he wants to win makes your feet somehow suddenly race for the bench.

Let me give you a hockey example of why this guy inspires me.

One winter, Cam, Mike Fox, a close friend of ours named Jim Pallotta, and I decided to play two-on-two hockey. This particular morning the weatherman said it was five degrees outside with a wind chill factor that made it feel like minus seven. Of course, to maniacs like us, a wind chill of minus seven means just one thing: it's pond hockey time.

Jim's an Italian American with working-class roots in Boston's famed North End, and a fantastic athlete. We were on a trip with our wives and had brought our hockey bags along. So out on a frozen sheet of midwinter Vermont ice, it was strictly Old School Hockey: no helmets, just shin guards and gloves.

We paired up as USA versus Canada in a best of seven series, first team to hit a small wooden log in the net five times wins each match. The advantage was definitely in Team USA's favor. Jim and I were both healthy and in great skating shape. Cam was hampered by his severely arthritic right hip, which would soon have to be replaced, and a balky knee that limited his turning radius.

And Mike, of course, had Parkinson's.

But the air was crisp, the sky was blue, and the friendships ran deep as we skated back and forth for six fun games, laughing and hustling to a 3–3 tie. We could have stopped there. It had been a great two hours, we were all getting hungry, and it was easy to see that Cam was in pain and Mike's medication was wearing off. That's when Cam said:

"You good to go, Mike?"

Cam had that famous look in his eyes, and it lit Mike up. "Oh yeah. I'm ready to roll," Mike responded.

"Game seven, right now," Cam barked. "Let's go!" And go we did.

Right from the opening face-off, Jim and I were on our heels as the thought of losing transformed Team Canada into a tornado. Cam was barreling around blocking shots and racing after rebounds. Jim and I were struggling to get close to their net. We could see how limited Cam's skating range was, but his will to win wiped out the ache in his hip and leg.

Meanwhile, Mike had turned into a Parkinson's-infused water bug. It's hard enough to cover small fast guys in any contact sport—you can't hit what you can't catch—but it's absolutely impossible to read which direction an angry Parkinson's patient on skates is going to go. Head fakes and eye fakes are part of any hockey player's arsenal of tricks when carrying the puck, but Fox had so many moves going at once that he almost sent MY brain into seizures. His elbow twitches, leg spasms, shoulder shakes, and hand flutters had me reacting like a confused and uncoordinated rag doll.

Pallotta turned into an NHL defenseman, sliding and diving to stop shots, stealing the puck, and making impossible tape-to-tape passes to me. Neely was doing the same at Canada's end of the ice, sending Mike Fox flying for our net.

They went up 3–2 until Jim and I tied it. Then they went up 4–3 until Jimmy scored again. Now it was basically sudden death overtime. Team USA was sucking cold wind. Team Canada was doing the same. Again, we could have called it right there. But instead, I stole the puck from Cam and was headed up ice toward Mike Fox on defense when BOOM! I suddenly found myself flying through the air and BAM! stuck face-first in a snowbank. The result of an arthritic hip check from Cam, who now had the puck and saucered a ridiculously beautiful pass over Jim's outstretched stick that Mike one-timed into the wooden log for the game-winning goal. I swept the snow off my face as Cam raised his hands like he'd just won the Stanley Cup.

Final score in the series: CANADA 4, USA 3.

That drive to conquer all odds is the reason Cam thinks one day the final score in his fight against the disease that stole his parents will be NEELY FOUNDATION 4, CANCER 0.

It's also how—as president of the Boston Bruins—he steered the team to a Stanley Cup victory in 2011. Just like on that day in Vermont, this guy never gives up the fight.

Dear Cancer: Better keep your fucking head on a swivel. Cam Neely's got your number.

* * *

In the weeks following the 9/11 attacks on New York City, Jane Rosenthal and her business partner Robert De Niro dealt with its aftermath on a daily basis. Their company Tribeca Productions was located a few blocks from the World Trade Center site, and De Niro not only still lived in the neighborhood, but was born there and had grown up walking those very same streets.

As the air slowly began to clear and the digging for lost souls continued, Jane and Bob watched as local businesses began to suffer. Restaurants and bars, art galleries and clothing stores, small markets and coffee shops were on the verge of closing forever as customers dwindled and the tourist trade disappeared. People were no longer visiting downtown Manhattan, some due to fear and others by assuming nothing was open.

I was down there a lot in those days, and I can tell you firsthand how silent the streets were—and how odd it was to sit in a restaurant where almost all of the other tables were empty. Night after night, day after day. Except for the ongoing recovery work at Ground Zero, Tribeca was a ghost town. Little Italy was deserted. Chinatown had no customers.

So Jane and Bob decided to do something about the situation. Not because they had to, but because they wanted to.

Engaging the help of Jane's husband at the time, Craig Hatkoff, the trio called in a bevy of celebrity friends and announced a restaurant crawl through downtown. Diners would show up at different establishments and eat side-by-side with famous people as they helped to spread the word that these great places were not only still open, but in dire need of financial salvation. Bob stopped in at each place to personally greet everyone and take pictures. Jane made sure the timing came off without a hitch. The press showed up to take photographs and write about the event.

And it worked.

Soon people from all over Manhattan were streaming south and helping to save businesses belonging to their fellow New Yorkers. Using this opportunity on an even bigger scale, a month later Jane, Craig, and Bob decided to start the Tribeca Film Festival, launching it with little more than a dream and their cell phones.

Again, not because they had to—but because they wanted to.

Working endlessly, calling in favors from all ends of the film world, reaching out to corporations and business connections for sponsorship and support, they quickly mounted a program of movies, speaking appearances, musical performances, and celebrity red carpets that filled up a week's worth of festivities.

Debuting in the spring of 2003, it was an immediate success—drawing even more attention and money to the neighborhood's recovery. At once exhausted and excited about what only a few months previously had seemed an impossible task, the trio decided to make the festival an annual event. Fifteen years later, it's not only one of the world's leading annual film celebrations, it has grown to include television and all forms of digital communication technology, and is responsible for rejuvenating downtown New York and bringing over nine hundred million dollars back into the city's economy.

But Jane and Bob didn't stop there.

They joined forces with other city luminaries to raise funds for the National 9/11 Memorial & Museum, devoting even more time and energy to that cause as board members, and helping to complete one of the most moving and detailed tributes to those who gave their lives on that horrible day. It took more than ten years to complete, but I can tell you as someone who has walked through it, the experience is not only unforgettable but also holds a special healing power.

The Tribeca Film Festival happens each and every spring in downtown Manhattan. The National 9/11 Memorial & Museum is open every day in the shadow of One World Trade Center, also known as the Freedom Tower. Jane and Bob's Tribeca Productions is still located in its original building a few blocks away. In the same neighborhood their charitable spirit helped save.

Not because they had to. Only because they wanted to.

*   *   *

In the summer of 1995, Lenny Clarke was a miracle of modern science: addicted to cocaine and yet weighing 388 pounds. He could suck down half a gram and an entire pizza in less than thirty minutes. Which he did on an almost daily basis.

Needless to say, Lenny was not a scientist.

One of comedy's shooting stars back in the late eighties—performing in sold-out arenas with Sam Kinison and headlining his own critically acclaimed eponymous CBS sitcom—he had adopted Sam's drug and food habits as his own. The two of them even started a temporary food and drug delivery service when their show business mentor Rodney Dangerfield was forced into a weight loss clinic by his third wife. Sam and Lenny would sneak pizza, weed, and blow to Rodney through a side alley door each evening.

They were the angels of evil.

But ultimately, for Lenny, marrying his own coke dealer and spending money as if there was no tomorrow led to heartbreak and financial problems that he couldn't overcome once his TV show got canceled. Sam's tragic early death in an automobile accident only sent him further out on the limb of edgy behavior. His drinking became uncontrollable, and the cocaine and food electrons that fired through his woozy brain now read as inconceivable science fiction: an entire gram of blow followed by a hotel room service tray of five shrimp cocktails, two orders of French fries, three filet mignons that he ate like meat donuts, plus a serving bowl full of whipped cream and two containers of Häagen Dazs. Any flavor.

All followed by one of his famed medical inventions: the NyQuil

Stinger. I was around for the creation of that particular prescription, back in 1982. It was Lenny's solution for falling asleep after a long night of cocaine abuse.

We lived on the same block, and many a night I was the designated driver as we headed home from a comedy gig. One time Lenny made me stop at a twenty-four-hour pharmacy as he purchased two bottles of NyQuil. When I asked him who had a cold he said, "Me. I got the cocaine flu. But half a bottle'a this mixed with four fingers of whiskey and I'll not only sleep like a baby, but when I wake up tomorrow my sinuses'll be crystal clear."

Ladies and gentlemen: meet Dr. Lenny Clarke.

There are a ton of insane stories about Lenny floating around out there—and I'm here to tell you that every single one of them is true:

At age fifteen he set the single-season record for sneaking into Fenway Park: thirty-seven times. Which is amazing, given how loud and rambunctious Lenny is at any sporting event. The ushers must have been deaf.

At age eighteen he was a fantastic football player and a straight C-minus student with little hope for a college scholarship. One of his sisters was engaged to a black guy Lenny looked up to, who informed him that he'd gotten a full college ride based on affirmative action. So Lenny, a quick learner in spite of his grade point average, filled out a state college application. Next to the question asking his ethnicity, he listed *African American*. And sure enough got a full ride. Nobody seemed to notice that fall as he settled in on campus and kept a low profile. Everything was going fine. Until he decided to run for president of the freshman class.

Now you know why he got all those C-minuses.

At age twenty, he applied to be a lead-paint inspector in his hometown of Cambridge, Massachusetts, basing his qualification for the job on the fact that he'd eaten tons of lead paint chips as a small child in the housing project where he grew up. "I know what the stuff actually tastes like," he explained. "Who else you got here has THAT skill?"

At age twenty-four, while working as a janitor at city hall, he decided to run for the Cambridge City Council after finding out the government had to give matching funds to anyone who declared themselves a candidate and got a hundred people to sign a petition of support. He got the signatures and used his funds to print up FUCK THE KENNEDYS—VOTE FOR LENNY CLARKE bumper stickers. The Kennedys were not involved in this particular political contest. Lenny just wanted to get everyone's attention. Which he did. The city council asked for their money back. He then ran on a promise to clean up city hall.

During that same election, he stole a city bus and drove around to random bus stops picking people up and driving each of them right to their front doors, all the while asking for votes while making them laugh their asses off. The whole thing ended in a police chase. And Lenny finishing fifteenth out of thirty-six candidates, while being allowed to keep his janitorial job, proving there's no such thing as bad publicity AND that Lenny Clarke is a man of his word.

At age thirty-three, his affection for cocaine reached the point where he felt a burning curiosity to research how the product was manufactured. So he flew to Colombia and started asking around. They thought he was a cop. End of research. He stayed for a week and drank his hotel out of whiskey and tequila.

At age thirty-five, he invented an alcohol concoction named the Lenny Clarke Carnival, a nod to his talent for always winning the top shelf prize in amusement park shooting games. The Carnival is still available today. Here's how you can get one: walk into any drinking establishment and tell the bartender to take a pint glass and pour equal amounts of all the expensive booze bottles on the top shelf into it. Once the bartender hands you this expensive mixture, you down it in two gulps. Maybe three.

I sipped a Carnival once. Know what it tasted like? NyQuil. The original Green Death flavor.

Warning: do not ingest cocaine and pizza after drinking the Lenny Clarke Carnival. Unless your name is Lenny Clarke.

At age thirty-seven, Lenny informed me that he'd read his first book. Which was *Merv,* the best-selling autobiography of talk show host and game show creator Merv Griffin. Someone had left it on an airplane and Lenny read it cover-to-cover while flying from L.A. to N.Y. on a red-eye coke binge. This would not only qualify him as a speed reader but also quite possibly the least informed friend I'd ever had.

When I asked him how he got through high school without ever reading a single thing, he admitted he was dyslexic—the words and letters he saw on paper or the blackboard became jumbled and switched around. In order to memorize lines for his sitcom he had to pace back and forth on a beach while his ex-wife read the lines out loud and he implanted the dialogue into his brain. The flight back from L.A. was the first time in his life Lenny was able to read something word for word. So in a strange way, Lenny actually WAS a doctor. Because he unearthed a major medical breakthrough: cocaine cures dyslexia.

At age forty-four, Lenny was acting in an independent film being

shot in Boston, showing up on time for work each day but partying his fat ass off every night. On the final day of shooting, when
a fellow actor mentioned the wrap party that was taking place
that very night at an old church, Lenny bought an eight ball of
blow and a pint of whiskey and headed on over. Having been at
the famed Limelight club in New York City, Lenny thought it was
about time Beantown had an old church that was turned into
a disco. Figuring this party would be an all-night rave, he had
rigged his coke in a small glass bullet bottle for easy access. Upon
entering the church club, he saw about two hundred people in
the pews and took a seat in the back, sucking down some booze
while sucking up some nose candy. There was a guy standing at
the pulpit explaining what Lenny thought were the party rules:

"My name is Bobby and I'm an alcoholic."

The crowd responded as one: "HELLO, BOBBY!"

Holy shit, Lenny thought, *this is gonna be my kind of fucking
night—a whole room full of total party animals.*

As Bobby continued to talk about drinking a quart of whiskey
a day, using cocaine, getting into bar fights, and blacking out,
Lenny was very impressed. *I gotta meet up with this guy later on,*
he thought—*we are gonna be best fucking friends.* He did another
bump. Swallowed another shot.

Then Bobby mentioned the last time he had a drink or a drug.
Which was five years previously. Everyone applauded. Except
Lenny. He turned to a woman sitting next to him and asked:
"Hey, what time does the party start?"

She replied: "It never ends. That's why we're all here. This is a
meeting of Alcoholics Anonymous."

Lenny was aghast. He left in a huff, bitching to himself about the turncoat actor who played a prank on him. Back at his hotel, Lenny proceeded to drink and snort himself into oblivion.

The next morning, it all somehow sank in. An empty bottle of whiskey and the clumped remnants of white powder stuck to a tabletop were harsh signposts he'd woken up to a million times before. His face was a red wreck. His head was pounding. But in between pumping boozy blood through his cocaine-infested veins, his fatty heart stopped sinking as he suddenly came to realize: the actor had actually done him a favor. He tossed the bottle and took a long shower, thinking back on all the wasted days and brain cells.

That night he went back to the church, still hungover but completely sober, and sat in on his first full meeting as a member of Alcoholics Anonymous. It felt like a new beginning. (Don't worry—I got his permission to tell that story.)

He's been clean and sober for twenty years as of this writing. Not only that: he turned his whole life around. The moment of clarity he gained from that drunken church visit turned into a world tour: Lenny attends mass in churches around the globe whenever he's on location for a movie, TV show, or stand-up performance. He also donates countless dollars on each and every church visit.

After ten years of sobriety, Lenny also set out on a weight-loss program, ultimately dropping almost two hundred pounds. Today he is a svelte buck-eighty-five and a happy guy who has saved many lives by preaching the gospel of AA.

Including mine.

Ten years ago he helped me get sober, and has been a touchstone of guidance and support ever since. Whenever I reach out—in person or by phone—he's always there. And his unrelenting desire to help others has extended into many other avenues. He doesn't want me writing about that stuff, but you know what? Fuck him. I'm putting it down on paper to prove how a person can change through the power of a twelve-step program. This is a partial list of the organizations he helps raise money for every year, as well as hosting or performing at each group's annual charity events:

Massachusetts General Hospital, the Joey Fund, the Jimmy Fund, the Cystic Fibrosis Foundation, the Susan G. Komen Breast Cancer Foundation (now known simply as Susan G. Komen), the SEALS Family Foundation, the National Multiple Sclerosis Society, the Light Foundation, the Cam Neely Foundation for Cancer Care, the Michael J. Fox Foundation, the David Ortiz Children's Fund, the Boston Bruins Alumni Association, the McCourt Foundation, the Mark Bavis Leadership Foundation, the FDNY Foundation, the Leary Firefighters Foundation, and far too many more to list here.

His calendar is so jammed with charity events, he rarely has a week without one. I've personally never known an individual who donates as much of his time and energy to such kind and selfless work every single day of the year.

Plus, I'm pretty sure it's not really that selfless after all. I think he's trying to do a ton of good stuff now just to make up for the nine million bad things he did during the evil part of his life.

His answer to that charge?

"You bet your ass I am. If there IS a heaven, I wanna make sure I get a good seat."

* * *

My cousin Jerry Lucey's obituary described him as "a firefighter's firefighter"—the ultimate compliment that can be paid from one member of the fire service to another. Jerry served our hometown department in Worcester, Massachusetts, and gave his life in the line of duty on December 3, 1999, only a few city blocks from the Main South neighborhood where we grew up.

That day dawned cold and clear in Worcester. Jerry was working out of a downtown firehouse with Rescue One. Nearby, a guy who grew up across the street from me and was my classmate for twelve years at Saint Peter's Catholic School was leading Ladder Two that night: Lieutenant Tommy Spencer. Some thirty-plus guys from the old neighborhood had chosen to become members of the Worcester Fire Department, answering the call to save others as their full-time job.

Meanwhile, two homeless people had holed up in an abandoned building near the elevated expressway just a short distance from both firehouses. The Worcester Cold Storage Warehouse was a brick behemoth—six stories high and occupying one full city block. It had no windows above the second floor, and inside it was a maze of connected meat lockers, the walls and ceilings coated with layers of cork, tar, expanded polystyrene foam, and spray-applied polyurethane. It was flammable to supreme levels. So when the couple knocked over a candle and some nearby newspapers caught fire, it escalated quickly.

They made a split-second decision to run away.

Meanwhile, an off-duty firefighter traveling down the expressway noticed gray smoke coming from the roof and called it in. Moments later Rescue One, Ladder Two, and Engine Three responded. Pulling up to the building and hearing from a local business owner and witness that two homeless people had recently been seen squatting there, they ran inside. Jerry and his partner Paul Brotherton led a search of the upper floors. Several other firefighters looked through the bottom three. Chief Mike McNamee described what happened next:

> There was a light smoke condition in the upper levels of the building, to the point where we didn't even have our face pieces on. Within four seconds it went from that to hot, black boiling smoke.

He called for everyone to immediately exit the building. A head count revealed that Jerry and Paul were missing. They radioed for help, confused about their exact location. Tommy Spencer then insisted on rushing in with firefighters Jay Lyons, Joe McGuirk, and Tim Jackson alongside him to find Jerry and Paul. Moments later, the building exploded into what would be described as a massive brick oven of smoke and flame. The top four floors collapsed down onto the first two.

And all hell broke loose.

The building became an inferno. A surge of ladder companies and engine teams rolled in and shot water at a blaze that burned for days on end. The massive orange flames and rancid smoke filled the skies for miles around. It took a full week and a half to put out the fire and find the bodies, with teams of firefighters arriving from around the country—and the world—to dig into the hot stack of rubble. In the coal-black winter nights, in the icy blue December days, an army of firefighters sifted through the steaming ash in search of bone fragments, the steel heads of scorched axes, teeth, badges—any sign of their fallen brothers.

With Christmas just around the corner, this frigid battle they fought captured the attention of Americans from every corner of the country. Money poured in from each state, with individuals and organizations reaching out to help the widows and family members. Messages of support and prayers for discovery were daily arrivals. Bags of letters and envelopes containing checks and cash were sorted at fire headquarters. Each night became a desperate wait for the end of a story everyone already knew to be deeply, tragically sad.

In a true display of the vast brotherhood that bonds firefighters together, men from departments far and wide worked 24/7 in shifts full of brute strength and fine detail—literally moving a broken brick mountain inch by horrible inch, refusing to quit until they found evidence of Jerry, Paul, Tommy, Joe, Jay, and Tim.

The national media came to call them the Worcester 6. Their memorial service at the Worcester Centrum was attended by 14,000 people inside the arena, and 25,000 more outside. President Clinton and Senator Ted Kennedy eulogized them as heroes. American flags were majestically folded and offered to their wives and parents. It was a somber yet spiritually uplifting goodbye.

Some firefighters describe heavy fire as "the bitch," and it was that type of challenge Jerry loved most. He was a truck guy—in fire department terminology that means the people who run in first. The rescue teams. The bravest of the brave. But on December 3, 1999, all six of these men displayed a courage few of us have within our hearts—searching for missing citizens in a torching terror of heat and smoke, then going on a more dangerous mission to save each other under even worse conditions.

They left behind an entire nation praising such remarkable valor. They also left seventeen children without fathers.

Jerry died doing what he loved best. Firefighting wasn't just a job for him, it was his life's calling. He was an active presence on the Massachusetts Fire Department Hazardous Waste Material Team, a proud member of the Worcester Fire Department Honor Guard, and a teacher at the Massachusetts Firefighting Academy. When he wasn't spending time with his wife, Michelle, and two sons, Jerry and John, he was helping other firefighters get better training and finding new ways to improve his own performance skills.

Jerry's legacy lives on in his son Jerry, who is now a member of the Worcester Fire Department. Four of Paul Brotherton's sons are also Worcester firefighters. So is one of Tommy Spencer's boys. Six new young men in bunker gear, inspired by the passion of their dads. There's a wonderful symmetry in such a devoted tribute.

Meanwhile, the Worcester Cold Storage Warehouse has been replaced with a new firehouse on the same site, from which Rescue One still races to alarms each and every night. That may be the greatest tribute of all. Because it's exactly how Jerry would want to be remembered. There is a marvelous stone and bronze monument to the Worcester 6 in front of that firehouse, but the doors flying open and the rigs roaring out speaks more closely to the heart and soul of my cousin.

If he had survived the Worcester Cold Storage Warehouse Fire that freezing December night, if he had walked out of the building alive and another alarm sounded for a second fire in a nearby three-decker, he would have pulled up, jumped off the rig, and been the first guy to run inside.

It's who he was. A man of action. A beast in the bitch. A firefighter's firefighter.

* * *

There you have it: twelve Americans who changed the communities they live in. Who managed to do good deeds when faced with personal demons, tremendous odds, and even death. People who decided to overcome obstacles by offering up their time—their blood, sweat, and tears—to make a difference.

I'm not going to tell you which political candidates they voted for or which parties they may have supported now or in the past. Some of them you can Google. Some of them you can't. And some of them, I never even thought of asking.

Because none of that bullshit matters.

Fire doesn't care who you voted for. Parkinson's doesn't attack based on political affiliation. Cancer is out to kill everyone on both sides of the aisle.

Disease, disaster, and physical disability are all bipartisan issues. They suck. Hard. These twelve people have already made them suck way less than they used to.

Try and filibuster THAT.

If one morning I left the Oval Office, headed down to the Potomac River, and walked across the top of the water, all the way to the other side—the headline that afternoon would read "President Can't Swim."

—LBJ

FAKE NEWS, REAL GUNS

During the last election cycle, a man from North Carolina with an Internet addiction and a history of drug and alcohol problems believed the online Fake News theory claiming John Podesta and Hillary Clinton were running a pedophile sex slave operation out of a Washington, D.C., pizza shop. So he drove seven hours to Comet Ping Pong, entered the restaurant, and fired several shots from his AR-15 before being subdued by police.

The subsequent Real News headlines were all about how insane it was for someone to buy into such a clearly false Fake News story. How about the insanity of the same idiot being able to buy a gun? The real headline should have been ANOTHER TOTAL MORON GAINS ACCESS TO MILITARY-GRADE WEAPONS.

This doesn't bode well for our future, folks. We are entering an era where part of the population can't find factual information but knows EXACTLY where to locate assault rifles with giant mags of ammunition.

In America, you still have to take the SATs to get into college. Even a junior or community college. How about we require a simple IQ test before you purchase a gun? Some sample multiple-choice questions:

I AM BUYING A GUN TODAY BECAUSE:
A. I can
B. Fuck you
C. Nancy Pelosi is making meth in a D.C. McDonald's bathroom

THE SECOND AMENDMENT IS:
A. Our constitutional right to bear arms
B. Fuck off
C. New show from Netflix

"WE THE PEOPLE" IS A FAMOUS PHRASE FROM:
A. The Constitution
B. Go fuck yourself
C. Mark Wahlberg

The mainstream media is not the enemy of the American people. Mentally unhinged Americans on the Internet are. Conspiracy con man Alex Jones spread the Comet story on his Infowars website week after week during the 2016 election, and then apologized afterward in a six-minute video blaming third-party rumors and "reporters who are no longer with us." Those so-called reporters are actually just on-set hired hands who scour the Internet for crazy theories, print them out, and place the pages in front of Alex. Who then randomly decides which ones fit into his daily feverish media feed.

Appearing on NBC for a seated interview with Megyn Kelly this past June, a sweaty and twitch-ridden Jones fumbled to explain away the Ping Pong fuckup and his belief that the mass shooting of twenty children and six adults at the Sandy Hook

Elementary School in Newtown, Connecticut, was a hoax created by gun control advocates. After Megyn's eerily too-calm questioning, an angry Jones reacted by accusing her of having an agenda.

Here's a real news headline for you, Alex: EVERYBODY IN THE MEDIA HAS AN AGENDA.

Megyn Kelly's was to showboat the Infowars insanity on network television for big Sunday-night ratings. Alex's agenda is to scare the shit out of as many Americans as possible so he can sell us his latest website products: gas masks, survival seed vaults, bulletproof backpacks, and other tactical gear you'll need for impending Armageddon—plus a full array of weight-loss supplements.

Although let's be honest, Alex. If we're planting Infowar Survival Seeds and swallowing Alex Jones Anti-Radiation Pills in what may remain of the woods after a biological terror attack? Our belly fat will be the first thing to go.

New idea: Alex Jones Apocalypse Abs! Meet your maker looking like you did in your high school heyday! Slim down for good before you check out forever!

Alex believes the government controls our weather with special weapons that can create tornadoes and hurricanes. He also believes government forces blew up the Twin Towers on purpose. Not to mention their ongoing plans to turn America gay. "The reason there are so many gay people now," Alex explains, "is it's a chemical warfare operation." He claims the government is lining juice boxes, water bottles, and potato chip bags with secret formulas that feminize men. And he's been obsessed by the military's development of a "gay bomb" so powerful it can even turn frogs into homosexuals.

Maybe those Apocalypse Abs are just part of a plot to make Alex more attractive after Armagayddon.

None of this would matter except for one thing: our current president is an Alex fan. From the Obama Birther Theory to an ocean of HILLARY FOR PRISON T-shirts, Trump has ridden the Crazy Alex Train for all it's worth, while constantly deriding any actual journalist who criticizes his White House actions. Trump reacts to every negative article written about him with the fragile aplomb of a sensitive thespian.

Listen, Mr. President: I get it.

I've been working in the theater, concert arenas, and on-screen for all of my adult life. I still remember the first positive reviews I received from our college newspaper after the Emerson Comedy Workshop made its stage debut in 1976: glowing remarks about all of us, but also singling me out for a bit about smoking, a rant against rock stars, a sketch concerning breasts of many sizes, and a satirical song called "Chainsaw Love." All the pieces of my No Cure for Cancer comedy persona were already in place.

I don't recall the actual words from the article. Just the positive vibe. But I do remember phrases from my first negative review a couple of years later. And several from the beginning of my movie career. And the middle. With specific words that still remain in my head. A sampling:

"Not funny and not fun."
"Spiky-haired hipster."
"Dead on arrival."
"Inane and inept."
"Why are they still making Denis Leary movies?"
"Rescue Me from watching his long, horsey face."

I typed each of those from memory. That's how emblazoned they still are in my brain. Can't recall what I had for lunch yesterday but the six arrows above are still stuck like knives in my neural structure.

It happens to everyone in public life.

I remember having a wild conversation on the set of *Wag the Dog* about this when Dustin Hoffman recited his worst review from *The Graduate*—word for word—thirty years after it was printed. And Willie Nelson recalled a couple of specific sentences that Nashville music critics used to denigrate his voice, face, and songwriting talent at the beginning of his career. Two Hall of Fame–level, Grammy-winning, Oscar-owning entertainers with reams of positive press written about them but only able to remember the worst of the worst.

It's human nature to focus in on the detrimental. And in my case—as with Dustin and Willie—use it to fuel the fire. To say "fuck you" and keep on climbing.

Because number one: grabbing a public microphone to call out your critics by name only proves how much they mean to you— transferring the power into their inky, idle, ungifted hands.

And number two: maybe they're right.

My experience has been that after the initial shock and anger of a bad review, you learn within days if it's true or not. Because if ten other reviews come out and all say you suck, maybe you do. Temporarily, at least. On the other hand, if nine reviews come out and say you're a genius—that's not gonna last very long either.

There isn't an actor, singer, athlete, or politician you can name who hasn't had peaks and valleys in their careers. So I never went on *Letterman* and called *Entertainment Weekly* a fake magazine. I also didn't walk out onto Craig Ferguson's set with a copy of *The New York Times* so I could read a great review of mine out loud. Do I still cringe when bad reviews occur?

No.

Because I stopped reading reviews. I'm sixty years old. What the fuck are they gonna say—positive or negative—that I haven't already heard? I suck? Hear it at home when I forget to load the dishwasher. I'm great? Hear that at home when I load the dishwasher and do the laundry.

Donald, you are the leader of the free world: grow the fuck up. (I can't even believe I just typed that sentence to a seventy-one-year-old man.) In case you've forgotten, here's a sampling of the news organizations you have labeled as fake in the last three years, in your own words:

"CNN is fake news."
"*New York* magazine is a piece of garbage."
"The BBC has no credibility whatsoever."
"The Huffington Post is fraudulent."
"Fox News is totally biased and disgusting."
"NBC news is very dishonest."
"MSNBC? Please. A disaster."
"CNBC is crazy."
"The *New York Post* does false reporting."
"*Time* magazine is biased."
"*Meet the Press* is totally dishonest."
"ABC cannot report the news truthfully."
"*Saturday Night Live* isn't funny anymore."

That last statement was made about six months after you hosted the show and called it "fabulous." And you praised *Time* magazine this year when they put you on their cover as Person of the Year. Just two examples of how tender and elastic your ego can be. It's fake news when you don't like it, and real news when you do.

And the hilarious thing is, you used to create fake news about yourself by calling up New York's gossip columnists using a fake voice and fake name—and planting fake items about who you were fake fucking! You also hung framed copies of a fake 2009 Time magazine cover featuring a fake photo of your face and a fake headline reading THE "APPRENTICE" IS A TELEVISION SMASH! in the hallways of several Trump golf clubs.

In the words of Chris Berman and Mike Ditka: C'mon, man!

You're better than this. Even if you're not, fake it.

As evidenced by the LBJ quote that opens this chapter, every president has to endure negative jabs. It comes with the territory. Canceling the traditional POTUS appearance at the White House Correspondents' Dinner just reinforces the idea that you have no sense of humor about yourself.

Bad math, brother.

The last two Oval Office members who refused to laugh about themselves and their situation were named Nixon and Carter.

I feel confident saying these things to you because I know if they don't get published in 140 characters or less, you'll never actually read them.

And since you won't, back to the people who bought this book: The thing is, folks, it's fairly easy to identify fake news. Fake headlines would leap right off your computer screen: TRUMP ADMITS TO TINY PENIS or HILLARY BLAMES HERSELF.

Otherwise, it's all bullshit. Rachel Maddow hates Trump. Sean Hannity blows him on-air every night. They both serve up ideology instead of actual news. Talk about an echo chamber— millions of Americans turn on their TV just to hear their own beliefs reinforced forever. Literally going round in the same self-satisfying circle.

Where's the middle ground?

Anderson Cooper and Chris Wallace. Megyn Kelly and Shepard Smith. They deliver detailed reporting without snarky partisan sidebars. If your name is Kellyanne Conway and Anderson eye-rolls you live on CNN, it's not because you're a woman. It's because you are spewing fake facts from an alternative universe.

He lives on planet earth. You circle an orange sun.

Which is where alt-media comes in. With eight million news options online and another partisan batch on-screen, each body politic can end up ingesting only what it wishes to find. If you take an audience of white supremacists and feed them white supremacy news from white supremacist reporters, you don't get real news. You get conspiracy theories.

I don't believe in white supremacy. Why? I've seen us dance. To Coldplay and Kenny G.

The thing is, every single second of every single day you can find news that fits your political needs. They know this. "They" being: the various political companies who need to create different political clickbait that will drive you to their contrasting political websites where advertisers sell the exact same products to everyone.

I just Googled "Trump Should Resign." First headline up is from a site called PoliticusUSA and it reads SHOCKING POLL SHOWS MAJORITY WANT TRUMP TO RESIGN IF HIS CAMPAIGN COLLUDED WITH RUSSIA. Okay, first off? Crappy writing. The headline feels longer than the story below it. Second of all, the other headlines on the site's front page include:

KELLYANNE CONWAY FALLS FLAT ON HER FACE

RUSH LIMBAUGH FALLS APART

TRUMP HAS MENTAL COLLAPSE AT PRESS CONFERENCE

RED STATE STUPIDITY CONFIRMED

I did not make that last headline up. That's how insanely one-sided this site is. And the top three ads on page one are:

NEW PAIN-FREE LASER HAIR REMOVAL

3 SIGNS OF A FATTY LIVER

WIN FREE TICKETS TO SEE U2

When I Google "Obama Wiretapped Trump," Breitbart pops up first. Here are the headlines:

MEDIA DARLING OBAMA SILENT ON TRUMP WIRETAPPING

ALABAMA PASSES BILL EXTENDING "STAND-YOUR-GROUND" TO ARMED CHURCHGOERS

LENA DUNHAM SAYS UNBORN BABY A PARASITE GROWING INSIDE YOU

GENDER-BENDING BERKELEY MURDER SUSPECT WANTS TO BE REFERRED TO AS "THEY"

And the top three ads are:

5 PROSTATE CANCER SIGNS

ANGIOPRIM: THE SAFE WAY TO CLEAN
YOUR ARTERIES AND VEINS

LISTEN TO "WHATEVER IT TAKES" WITH HOST
CURT SCHILLING

Don't be a dunce. They are telling you what you want to hear about politics so you'll buy products that can save your private parts. Which is all harmless fun until some nimrod decides to man-up his bad info with an unregistered rifle.

Guns don't kill people—people kill people. They just do it a lot faster with the guns we have now. As in around three hundred rounds per minute. That's a lot of dead people. And the argument goes: *Hey, I need this type of weapon in case the bad guys break into my home.*

If you need an assault rifle that can fire that much ammunition to defend your home? You must be a horrible shot. Unless you're expecting multiple enemies with weapons as big as yours—in which case you have to be a giant fucking asshole.

I'm pro-gun and pro–gun control. And I'm not an anomaly. I believe in the right to bear arms, but I'm tired of hearing the NRA and other gun nuts pointing at the Second Amendment—and any moderation of it—as being commie-pinko-liberal propaganda. It's just common goddamn sense.

When you can no longer go see *Iron Man 4* without carrying two Glocks along with your popcorn, the answer isn't selling Raisinets and extra rounds.

When our children can't go to school without fear of getting shot, the solution isn't handing each kid a Kevlar vest and an AK-47.

When gun violence and deaths increase year after year, the cure isn't coming up with even bigger bullets.

No place is safe or sacred anymore. Not school, not work, not even church. And now they're coming after baseball. But the Steve Scalise shooting didn't result in tighter gun laws. It resulted in the NRA and its supporters asking to have every single member of the House and Senate fully armed with automatic weapons. This argument is offered up after every mass shooting in America: more guns and more bullets. If we give in to that gruesome urge, eventually everybody in America is gonna have to have a gat on them everywhere they go.

Including the ballpark.

Let's face it, folks: that might be our near future. The cycle of grief and astonishment we go through after each mass shooting grows shorter and more shallow as their frequency increases. So it's not that hard to imagine an America where we all have weapons 24/7. It might lead to a higher body count, but hey, look at the bright side: it would make baseball a helluva lot more exciting.

Think you're a tough out? Try stealing second base when the catcher is carrying. Not too many guys are gonna rush the mound if the pitcher has a pistol. You wanna slow trot around the diamond after a massive home run? You better be wearing a bulletproof batting helmet, pal. Let's arm the umpires, too.

Guys will play a lot fucking faster under threat of a flesh wound. Forget stats like Hit by Pitch. Hit by .44 Magnum will be way more impressive. We may one day hear Joe Buck say, "He's not just throwing heat out there, he's packing it."

And golf? I think it blows. But who wouldn't wanna watch if there were snipers hidden on random holes? Turbocharged golf carts and exploding balls. Nine irons and 9-millimeters. You could play all eighteen in less than an hour and a half. "What'd you get on that hole, Denis?" "A double bogey and some shrapnel in my shoulder." Trust me, no one's gonna waste time looking for a lost Top Flight when the woods are full of Smith & Wessons.

At the time our Founding Fathers created the Second Amendment, and specifically the right to bear arms, the only weapons available were muskets and cannons. Muskets shot one metal ball at a time. Each ball could only travel about seventy-five yards and was often apt to veer off wildly once it left the barrel of the gun. And muskets took almost a full minute to reload. In other words: they sucked. And so did your chances of survival. Because it only took about twelve seconds for your still-untouched target to run up and eviscerate you with his trusty old-fashioned sword.

Now, clearly the Founding Fathers would gladly take an assault rifle from any one of us if we flew back in time and handed them one. But saying a law written on December 15, 1791, should still apply word-for-word on December 15, 2017, is like saying today's drunk driving law should be the same as the one that existed in 1909. Spoiler alert: there was no law against driving drunk in 1909. There were also no stop signs, traffic lights, or seat belts.

You wanna go back in time to that kind of mayhem? I didn't think so.

We can keep on bemoaning the battalion of bullets that fly each time some psychopath gets his hands on a modern musket and takes out an army of innocent people, and then respond by constantly rearming ourselves. Or we can spend good money making it harder—if not impossible—for mentally deranged maniacs to get weapons of war. These people all seem to have the same backstory: lack of necessary medication. Problem is, they can walk into Walmart and buy a weapon anytime they want. But Zoloft? Whoa—slow down there, buddy. You gotta go see a doctor to get your hands on something THAT dangerous. In many states it's actually easier to buy a rifle than it is a bottle of Robitussin DM.

It's enough to make you have a massive anxiety attack every time you have to leave the house.

But fear not: we have some new drugs for that.

I never had a problem with drugs. I had problems with the police.

—KEITH RICHARDS

NEW DRUGS WE REALLY NEED

America has been on the cutting edge of prescription medication for decades. Creating pills to put down any demons that dare threaten our pursuit of happiness. And when pills won't work, the USA still has our back.

For instance, scientific and medical research have solved Seasonal Affective Disorder (SAD) by developing and prescribing the Light Therapy Lamp (LTL). You turn it on and sit near it for a few hours a day and voilà! Just feel the positive new vibes popping into your brain stem.

Here's a helpful hint: you don't need to buy any LTLs. Because you already have a ton of them in your house. They're called Fucking Lamps.

From here on out known as FLs.

Whenever modern medicine identifies a marketable disease, it automatically creates a cool, three-letter nickname to make it sound more serious. For instance, if enough of us complained that we no longer cared about anyone's opinion, and that seemed to be a problem for family members and friends? Within about six months, doctors would have a trademarked name as well as some pills—and a light fixture—to treat it with.

I'm calling it Zero Fucks Disease (ZFD). And I ain't seeking a cure.

As of this writing, the USA swallows 80% of the world's opioid supply. And 62% of that supply is legally obtained. The two most popular forms are OxyContin and Vicodin. Methadone came in a close third but fell asleep before the finish line.

We have so many people on doctor-prescribed opioids that, rather than wean patients off of them—which doesn't turn a profit—doctors are now developing new diseases based on the SYMPTOMS of opioid abuse. One of which has a cool-sounding name: OIC.

Opioid Induced Constipation.

Which is what killed Elvis. The King of Rock 'n' Roll was sitting on his master bathroom throne trying to take a shit when he died. Shame. If he could have just remained a living, breathing junkie for another forty years, 2017 would have moved his bowels for him. With the new miracle drug Movantik.

Yup, they actually put part of the word "move" right in the title.

Movantik makes your body take a giant crap. It also has a long list of side effects including headache, stomach pain, diarrhea, intestinal perforation, anxiety, irritability, sweating, chills, yawning, dizziness with fainting, and nausea with fainting.

Remarkably, OxyContin and Vicodin have the exact same list of side effects with only one difference: you can't take a shit.

Hello, Movantik.

God, if they had only approached cocaine and alcohol abuse this way. Then instead of talking aimlessly for hours on end (Cocaine Overabundance Condition) and burning off brain cells with booze (Alcohol Submersion Syndrome), I could have kept on partying until my kidneys gave out (Deficient Intestinal Kinesis).

Hey, motherfucker, I'm not some random drunken cokehead: I have COC, ASS, and DIK!

As long as America is curing its bathroom issues, we might as well solve several others that need to be addressed. So while you're waiting for ballooning TrobamaCare to morph into mysterious TrumpTaxIncentiveCare, you will at least be a happier and healthier person.

Mainly because you'll be high as a kite. High enough to develop ZFD.

As a celebrity doctor, I'm prescribing these:

BLAMEITALL
Are you having trouble at work?

Unable to stay in a lasting romantic relationship?

Do your family members and ex-friends tell you what a failure you are and why?

Guess what?

It's your own fucking fault!

Two pills a day and you will stop pointing fingers at your parents, the government, bad luck, and fate.

You'll come to realize it wasn't Obama who was holding you back—it was a giant case of denial with a legal-weed-and-Cheeto chaser.

You didn't vote for Trump and Pence. Or Clinton and Kaine. Nope. You chose the *Game of Thrones* and Apathy ticket.

No more aimless whining, no more pointless plans. Blameitall will solve it all.

Side effects include: getting off your fat ass and finally doing something.

ALTERNAFAX
Up is down! Wrong is right! Losing is winning!

And everyone adores you!

Spew fake data you just made up!

Like this: a new poll says 73% of Americans love your hair!

Who took the poll? YOU did! When? Who gives a fuck!

No side effects. Why? Because you said so!

MEXIGO
Makes illegal aliens realize what a mess this country is and urgently wish to deport themselves.

Side effects include: building a giant wall that keeps American tourists out of your birth nation.

And getting Eric Trump to pay for it.

CELLANOID

Cures the addiction to Facebook, Snapchat, Instagram, and every other idiotic social site or digital app.

Makes you only use your phone for what it really is: a fucking phone.

Side effects: eye contact and intimacy.

PHOBEGONE

Find yourself hating anyone who isn't white like you?

Afraid of minorities, gays, feminists, and the future? Don't worry!

Take one Phobegone tonight and wake up tomorrow loving every member of the LGBTQ community.

Not to mention straight women, black people, Jews, Mexicans, Muslims—hell, everybody on earth!

Side effects: Can't listen to Rush Limbaugh without puking.

CONSERVATOR

One dose a day and you'll not only know how to avoid paying taxes but believe every single thing that comes out of Sean Hannity's mouth.

Curse Ted Koppel!

Cherry-pick negative Obama video clips from nine years ago!

Build a Corey Lewandowski shrine in your backyard!

Side effects may include: a sudden desire to blow Scott Baio.

OBAMALENE
Restores your faith in hope and change.

Which actually no longer exist.

But you won't give a shit!

You'll be too busy giving wonderful speeches full of poetic phrases and handing out free health-care cards!

While you golf!

Side effects include: helping Hillary sell BERNIE WAS MY BITCH T-shirts outside the Chappaqua Starbucks.

BRONZITONE
You turn tan. Permanently.

And look just as vigorous and vital as our president.

Minus the tanning-bed goggle lines around the eyes.

Complimentary lavender lip gloss included. Along with a MAKE MAR-A-LAGO GREAT AGAIN hat.

No known side effects. Okay, one: You may have the urge to tweet random thoughts at 4:30 a.m. Fight them off with this:

TWITABAN
Kills the desire to tweet.

Instead, you actually read books and gain interesting and true historical information that makes you smarter.

Side effects may include: finger shrinkage, higher I.Q.

IVANKAPADE

Makes you sell, sell, sell—24/7/365. Shoes, scarves, dresses, and anything else you wear on *60 Minutes* or to a NATO summit.

Side effects: inability to smile while meeting the pope because he refused to buy a blouse—plus, his ring is bigger than yours.

COMADRIL

Places you in an eight-year-long sleep state so you can rest your sensitive bones and awake to the soothing sounds of our next president: Ted Danson. Or Ted Nugent. In either case, you can take another two-term dose.

Side effects include: sometimes answering to the name "Norm" and/or bowhunting liberals.

AMERICANE

It's just blow. But it comes in a red, white, and blue little bottle.

And you may not be in a coma but you'll feel so goddamn happy for the next four years you won't give a fuck who the president is. Prescription blow is medicinal marijuana's bigger, louder brother. And he loooooves to party!

Side effects: sudden death due to massive heart attack—but hey, if you voted for Hillary, that's probably a plus in your book right now.

First, God created man. Then He had a better idea.

—SISTER AGNES CATHERINE, 1973

IN GOD WE SUCK

We've all seen the bumper stickers and the hashtag with the letters WWJD. Meaning: What Would Jesus Do?

For one thing: not run for president and get elected in this country.

First of all, there's that murky relationship with the scandalous Mary Magdalene. And when that wasn't biting Him in the ass, there's another ripe territory for his opponents to point at: a thirty-three-year-old man who's not married and hangs around with twelve guys who follow Him wherever He goes? Sounds either too gay or too gangster for many voters.

And His liberal views on lepers and sinners will hurt Him in many conservative circles, not to mention feeding large crowds with free food. What is He? Some kind of socialist? And then there's that nickname: King of the Jews. Which means He can count on New York and California, but the rest of the country? Not so much. Jew-S-A! Jew-S-A!

And let's not forget about all the beards. People don't mind beards on baseball players, but when you're running for the highest office in the land a cabinet full of hairy-faced guys in togas and sandals just ain't gonna cut it. And even the voters in New York and L.A. will wince about the lack of women and black people in that posse.

This is before we even get into tax returns for a guy who hasn't held a paid position in His life. And what's His motto going to be? "Worship My Father"? Jesus would be denigrated as God's puppet. And I can just hear the TV pundits now:

"Too preachy."

"Too whiny."

"Bottomless jug of wine? Is this guy a candidate or a keyboard player?"

"Jethro Tull called. He wants his haircut back."

"I have one question for this supposed Son of God: Why isn't your Father running?"

If there is a God, I hope He's a She. Just to see the look on the faces of all the men who've spent centuries declaring war in His name when they show up at the Pearly Gates to find Her staring dolefully back at them.

Talk about an uh-oh moment.

Every single organized religion ever created on this planet has come up with rules to subjugate, repress, and control women. Their minds, bodies, and emotions. Not to mention birth cycles. Plus the right to vote, marry, and work. To this very day, women in America still fight for equal pay and consideration in business locations and government offices across the land.

I'M tired of it. And I have a penis.

The Bible, the Koran, the Torah—each is chock-full of rules and regulations that in so-called strict interpretation somehow manage to justify men killing each other in their chosen deity's name, but won't allow women to express an opinion.

Or show some leg. Or drive.

And every time we hold an election in the USA we have to listen to a tankload of bullshit from conservative candidates about what God wants for America and how God sees the law and why God hates gay marriage and blah blah biblical blah.

Here's the thing: it's 2017.

The geniuses who now want to uproot the separation of church and state built into our Constitution by the Founding Fathers are the same assholes who claim the Second Amendment can't be altered by one iota. They break open their Bibles and claim it answers every question ever asked. And it probably did.

Back in 1205 BC.

Which is apparently what year it still is in Henagar, Alabama. Where last March a woman named Carol Laney, owner of the Henagar Drive-In Movie Theater, raised a ruckus about Disney's latest live-action version of *Beauty and the Beast*.

Okay, I may have exaggerated when I said it was still 1205 BC in this town. But a drive-in? Sounds like Henagar's clocks got stopped during the Kennedy administration. The town's motto is "Building a Future, Preserving the Past." And they clearly ain't kiddin' about that second part.

After Carol booked the movie based on the poster, she was horrified to find out that the actor Josh Gad's character, LeFou, has what barely register as a few "gay" moments on-screen. When director Bill Condon announced that LeFou was, in fact, Disney's first officially gay character and a tribute to the lyricist Howard Ashman, who died of AIDS shortly after working on the animated original, Carol went off the rails and refused to show the new film.

Here's the statement she released:

> When companies continually force their views on us we need to take a stand. We all make choices and I am making mine. For those who do not know, *Beauty and the Beast* is premiering their first homosexual character. The producer also says at the end of the movie there will be a surprise for same-sex couples.
>
> This is by no means sending a message of hatred and bigotry; however, we are Christians first and foremost and must adhere to the Bible and its teachings. We hope you will come and support the Henagar Drive-In, maybe not for this movie but for others. Even though we do not condone the decision of the producers in *Beauty and the Beast* does not mean that we hate anyone. We know God will bless this endeavor.
>
> If we cannot take our eleven-year-old granddaughter and eight-year-old grandson to see a movie, we have no business watching it. If I can't sit through a movie with God or Jesus sitting by me, then we have no business showing it. I know there will be some who disagree with our decision. That's fine. We are first and foremost Christians. We will not compromise on what the Bible teaches.

First and foremost, I guess Jesus and God must really dig *The*

Boss Baby, Despicable Me 3, and *Hidden Figures,* which were all scheduled to play at Carol's Drive-In as of this writing.

Although it's a bummer Jesus and His Dad don't review movies in advance. Can you imagine what a box-office boost your family-friendly film would get if it received Four Halos from those two? Not to mention how great *No Halos* would be if you were marketing a twisted indie aimed at atheists.

Plus, *Jesus and His Dad at the Movies* is a kick-ass name for a film review TV show. The ratings would be yuge. I've got the advertising one-liner: "Watch us or die—your choice."

Second of all: back to Carol.

She must be a pretty fucking special lady if Jesus and God both request that they sit with her during *Ice Age 1* through 5. Religious zealots always think God is not only on their side, but literally AT their side. Musicians who thank God when they win a Grammy, actors who invoke the Lord as they clutch a trophy, baseball players who point at the sky and bless themselves after eking out a single, or George Bush Jr., who thought God was always speaking directly to him during his White House years.

If God were truly that involved in each of these lives, wouldn't it only make sense that Satan would have a hold on some public souls? I would love to listen to this postgame interview on ESPN: "I'd like to thank Satan for letting me hit that grand slam, and also for giving the other team's best reliever leukemia so I could face their backup guy."

My third point about Carol: she mentions that old standby "what the Bible teaches us"—which is religious code for "God hates gays." Or, at the very least, didn't create them. Or created them by mistake? I always get so confused when we get into this kind of religion-based science. And Carol makes it very clear that her decision "does not mean that we hate anyone."

Oh. Thank God. And His Son.

So it's not hate. It's just a massive amount of bigoted, backwoods fear.

That her granddaughter and grandson would somehow become homosexuals if they were exposed to an "alternative lifestyle" character in a major motion picture. Carol, let me update you on the most current mode of conversion therapy: everyone knows if your kids turn gay while watching a swishy Disney movie, you just rush them across town into a ballsy Jason Statham action flick and BOOM! They're back to being straight again. That's why we need Vin Diesel in the *Fast and the Furious* franchise: to keep our kids from doing musicals!

God forbid your grandkids see Josh Gad dancing for eight seconds when they could be watching Dwayne Johnson blow shit up for ninety-seven minutes.

Everything I love and hate about America is contained in Carol's story. A citizen using her right of free speech to silence the free speech of another citizen, while expressing her religious beliefs to throw shade at the sexual identity of an estimated fifteen million Americans. Give or take the two million conservative Christians who still haven't come out of the closet yet.

That last stat is me exercising my right to make a pretty safe assumption.

Shortly after shit-canning *Beauty,* Carol announced that her drive-in would be showing the movie *Fierce,* a story about British drag queens and their fight for equality. Sudden enlightenment on her part? Nope. Carol booked it based on the poster, which she said showed "a woman surrounded by dragons that made it look like a *Game of Thrones*–type thing."

She was shocked to find out it wasn't.

So Carol was fine with kids watching rape, incest, and beheadings, plus people being eaten by dogs or burned alive. Fire-breathing dragons yes. But fiery drag queens singing show tunes? How dare you.

Hey, Carol—I hate to break the news, but Disney movies have been chock-full of unofficially gay characters for decades now. The genie in *Aladdin,* Ken in *Toy Story,* same-sex couple Chip 'n' Dale, and possibly the entire cast of *Mary Poppins* have all struck a rainbow coalition chord with some discerning audiences. Think about it for a second: Mary hates Mr. Banks but crushes on his wife. Plus, Burt flirts with Mary far too much for a man who likes climbing filthy chimneys to join rooftop dance jams with twenty other guys. And let's not forget the glorious gay underpinnings of so many other animated icons: Ariel, Ursula, Belle, Mulan, Hades, Prince Eric, Terkina, Governor Ratcliffe, Oaken, Timon, Pumbaa, Elsa, and Dory. Whew.

Guess that puts a little crimp in your Christlike screenings.

Far be it from me to tell anyone how to live their lives, but hey—this is my book. And I'm getting tired of science as taught by people who don't believe in climate change or Neil Patrick Harris. And who only read one book written nine thousand years ago. So here I go: The Ten Commandments are not only out of date but almost impossible to completely obey.

Unless you're Faith Hill. Or a monk.

And they don't apply practically to modern American life any-more. But fret not, folks. I have an option. And it's specifically geared to the world we live in now:

THE TWELVE DEMANDMENTS
1. Thou shalt not kill.
2. Unless someone threatens to kill you first.
3. In which case, be my guest.
4. Thou shalt actively covet thy neighbor's spouse.
5. Let's face it: you're gonna do it anyway.
6. Just don't fuck him or her.
7. Google a porn star who looks like the person.
8. Have at it.
9. Help others. Not to Google porn. To eat, educate, and bet-ter themselves. Or to survive in times of crisis. Especially after natural disasters and during medical emergencies. Or even when they have a flat tire. It's called charity. Do it as often as possible. Why?
10. Because it will cancel out the killing and the coveting.
11. Don't be a douche.
12. Speaking of 11, don't try to sneak eleven items into the Ten Items or Less line. Even Jesus knows this is a dick move.

That's it. If you can't follow those simple twelve steps, then you're a piece of shit. And you can't be in my church. Which I'm call-ing Our Lady of Shut the Fuck Up. Each week we gather for an hour and listen to someone great make a speech on a subject we all need to learn more about. There is no texting, e-mailing, or Q and A afterward. No screaming over someone else because you don't like what they're saying. Shut the fuck up and listen. Thus the church title. When it comes to the Seven Deadly Sins, they also need to be dragged kicking and screaming into the current century. They were collected and enumerated by Pope Gregory I in 602 AD and almost immediately became a box-office bonanza. So much so that he was nicknamed Gregory the Great. Here's the official list, in descending nastiness, as he ranked them:

1. Pride
2. Envy
3. Wrath
4. Sloth
5. Greed
6. Gluttony
7. Lust

That's a *Game of Thrones* season finale. Or any episode of *Rescue Me*. And President Trump's tweets involve at least three of these sins per day. Me? I probably compose two to four sinful tweets per week. So let's call that a wash.

See? I employed one of the Seven Heavenly Virtues there: I cut Trump some slack. Never heard of the Seven Heavenly Virtues? Well, strap yourself in because a guy named Aurelius Prudentius came up with them in 410 AD—beating Greg the First's sin list by a couple hundred years. Here they are:

1. Modesty
2. Mercy
3. Grace
4. Passion
5. Charity
6. Prudence
7. Chastity

Sounds like the dance lineup from a really hip strip club.

Now, I did thirteen years in the Catholic prison system and I never heard one word about this Virtues thing. I asked around and none of my friends were aware of them either. That's because PG1 decided AP's goody-two-shoes approach was lame. For two solid centuries the Virtues weren't helping the Holy Vatican Bank get bigger revenues, and ol' Greggy figured out why: when it comes to religion, lowly sin sells way better than high self-esteem.

You can't nicely ask a Sunday congregation to please try harder at practicing the Seven Heavenly Virtues and then expect them to fork over their cash. Everybody in the crowd's gonna identify at least one Virtue they've used during the course of the last week. Plus, the words are all too happy: "virtue," "practice," "heaven."

That's a buyer's market.

But if you warn them in a scary voice to stop committing the Seven Deadly Sins before their evil souls burn in an eternal hell? They'll break out their wallets and beg for forgiveness with five-dollar bills. Thus did P Double G begin raising godly gazillions for Vatican City.

Fear, baby. That's what REALLY sells. Turning the Seven Heavenly Virtues into their exact opposites was a genius move. And which flick would you rather see? The one where Charlize Theron plays the modest and merciful social worker? Or the one where she's a hot spy in a miniskirt who kicks ass while flashing some sideboob? Put me down for the second. Which I'll watch at least three times.

Now, by my count, Carol Laney's statement contained two of the Deadly Sins—pride and wrath. But if she had practiced even just one of the Virtues—let's say mercy (kindness) or even some grace (patience)—she might have had the opportunity to listen and learn something about her different but still fellow human beings. Which is what I believe Jesus would have done.

Right after He finished watching *Captain Underpants*. With Carol.

At His favorite hangout: the Henagar Drive-In.

Now listen, I'm not pointing a finger. I'm GIVING the finger—BOTH of my middle fingers—to all the Bible-quoting, psalm-tweeting, evolution-denying, holier-than-thou amateur theists trying to make the rest of us kowtow to their personal beliefs. You have every right to express the notion that we should bow before this Big Voice in the Sky because some cute blond chick made it mad by taking a bite out of an apple eons ago. But the great thing about America is this: tons of us think that story sounds an awful lot like a Disney movie. And the Founding Fathers put a panic room in the political system to keep it safe from such animated ideology.

And by the way, it works. Especially when it comes to cash.

North Carolina is expected to lose four billion dollars in the next ten years due to the state government's ignorant refusal to recognize the bathroom rights of the LGBTQ community. That's gotta be the most expensive religious piss ever taken.

And just so you know, while I'm giving two middle fingers to the Bible fanatics, there's another eight fingers pointing right back at me. I ain't no angel. I got kicked out of the altar boys of Saint Peter's parish for drinking the Holy Wine and then demoted to the choir, where I lasted a few weeks. Until I got caught smoking in the choir balcony during a break between Palm Sunday songs. So in your eyes I'm already a goner. Plus, the Seven Deadly Sins read like a checklist of my adult afternoons.

ANY afternoon.

On any day of any week I could be driving my big truck with a boner for its bulk until I see a nicer truck with a cooler color than mine, which I forget about once the asshole driving it cuts me off, so I chase him down like a lunatic and give him the finger while challenging him to pull over and fight.

Two hours later I'm taking a couch nap after torquing down an Italian foot-long sub that I didn't offer any of to my wife, and forty-five minutes after that I'm awake and staring at this hot new Weather Channel chick who I think is predicting a hurricane but I'm too busy staring at her tits to tell.

Forgive me (which is a basic Christian belief) for not reading between the lines, but there ain't anything specifically against homosexuality on the Deadly Sins list. It also says nothing about cursing, so let's put a pin in that bullshit right now.

A team of researchers from around the world recently finished a study proving people who use profanity are less likely to be associated with lying or deception and also score higher on IQ tests.

Guess that explains why I'm a goddamn Doctor of Arts and fucking Letters, bitch.

And I'm not here to offend you: I'm trying to help. Instead of spending precious time covering your ears and writing letters drenched in religiously correct outrage about obscene words that endanger your pristine existence, listen to the facts.

Jack Grieve, a lecturer in forensic linguistics at Aston University in England, decided to spend an entire year studying how we curse in America.

Aston University is like Trump University, except for the fact that it has actual buildings with real classrooms where legitimate professors teach testable knowledge that leads to a legally recognized degree and educated skills that can get you a paid professional job.

So not the same at all, really.

Because of America's vast cultural canvas and our guaranteed right to freedom of speech—plus our much-envied use of that freedom all day, every day—we were the perfect test group. Grieve and his crew created a unique data-mining project using a massive corpus of geo-tagged tweets to measure and geo-code lexical innovations and interactions along with stratas of even deeper digital information.

As Professor Grieve said in a 2015 interview, "It takes a while to count through all the data, but then you have a big index with the relative frequencies per billion words for the top 60,000 most common words in English measured across the 3,000 counties in the contiguous United States (minus Alaska and Hawaii) and then run a local spatial autocorrelation analysis to help visualize the geographic clusters in the data."

In other words: we curse like fucking crazy.

God knows I curse enough to have a genuine interest in conducting a survey like this, but I've been a little busy working on *Ice Age 6* with Jesus and His Dad.

Plus, I suck at science. I believe in it and love reading results, but if I were in charge of doing an entire year examining numbers and stats? It would only work if we were researching the Boston Red Sox or how many "fucks" there are in a Martin Scorsese movie.

Here are Grieve's maps of the top eight American swears:

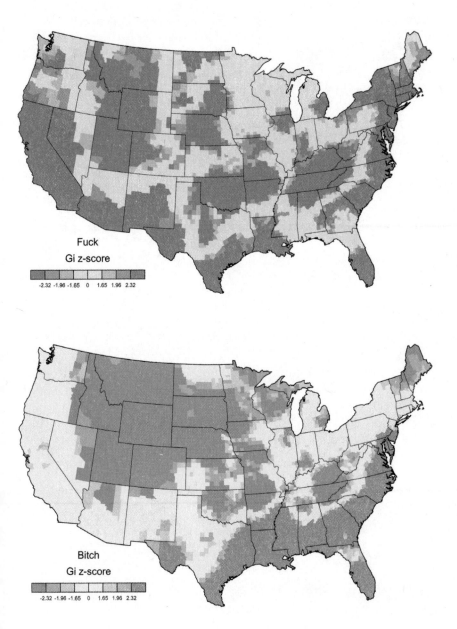

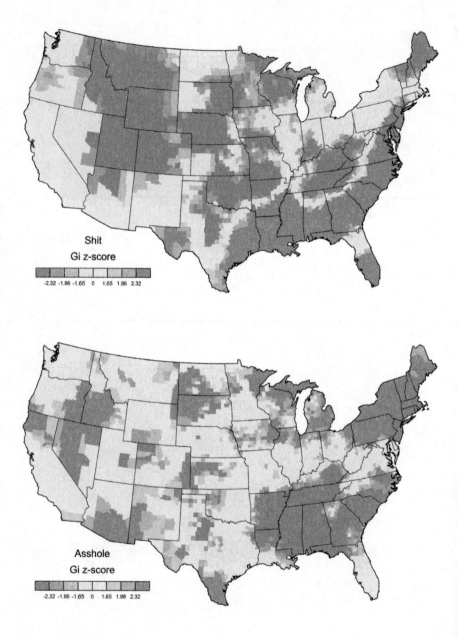

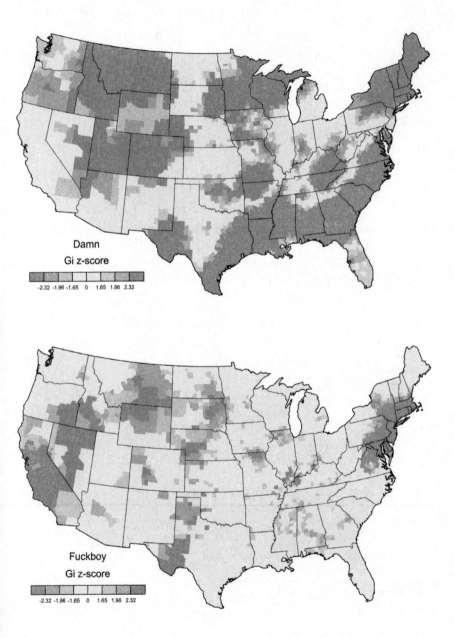

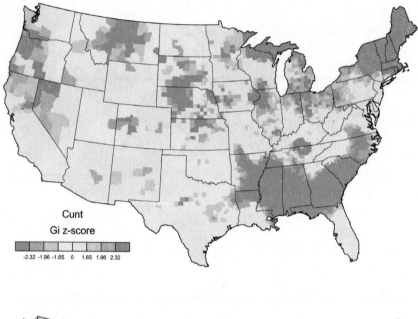

Cunt
Gi z-score

-2.32 -1.96 -1.65 0 1.65 1.96 2.32

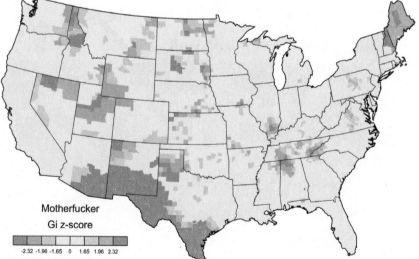

Motherfucker
Gi z-score

-2.32 -1.96 -1.65 0 1.65 1.96 2.32

And there you have it.

The one thing we all agree on: cursing our cocks off.

Fuck, Bitch, Shit, Asshole, and Damn cut across all voting cat-
egories. Red states, blue states—north, south, east, and west.
No matter how we vote on abortion and gun control—for or
against—we all use the same swear words to express our opinions about the two issues: *Fuck this shit, bitch.*

Not only that: we all clearly agree on hating the words Cunt and
Motherfucker.

But Fuckboy? Who saw that one coming?

I'm proud of the fact that amidst all of our political, religious,
and ethnic differences we somehow creatively joined brains to
add such a twisted new term to our national cussword vocabu-
lary.

Sure, it's a surprise that Bitch beat out Shit in a close race for
the second spot. And Asshole barely defeating Damn as they
fought it out at number four is a shocker as well: Vegas odds—
and mine—would have had Damn finishing much higher.

But Fuckboy?

A lot of us have been using it for ages, yet it's always been an
occasional choice. I've been called Fuckboy and I've called my
friends Fuckboy, but the instances are few and far between
when compared with something like Fuckface. Dr. Grieve even
called Fuckboy "the fastest-rising word on American Twitter."

So it's a bipartisan pleasure to welcome Fuckboy into the elevated bad language echelon that was once ruled by Damn,

which I would have expected to come in at least at number three given all its goddamned iterations. But as disappointing as Damn turned out to be, the real motherfucker here is Motherfucker.

I thought it was an easy top-five favorite. It had everything going for it: multiple syllables to trip off the tongue, significant sound elements for dramatic effect, and a long, successful career that raised the word above and beyond its literal meaning into usage as a noun, pronoun, adjective, and verb. But, alas, it was far too little, much too late. When you finish in last place, behind Cunt? That has to hurt.

And speaking of Cunt—I may have waited my entire life to type that last phrase. Why? Because I'm about to defend the curse word that came in seventh. First of all, the fact that it didn't finish last gives me hope. I love the word. Let me explain:

I grew up surrounded by Irish people, so when the nuns told us we couldn't say the c-word at school, we thought they meant "cocksucker." For the Irish, Cunt is akin to Motherfucker in its sweeping and dexterous linguistic powers.

Some examples:

"That car is a cunt."

"This cunty weather blows."

"He was cunting around down at the pub."

To the Irish, Cunt means everything EXCEPT cunt. "Fanny" is the Cunt of Ireland. Don't say it while visiting there. Ever. Don't talk about your fanny pack or mention Fannie Mae. Do NOT say, "My fanny hurts," or "You've got something stuck to your fanny."

Which brings us to the issue at hand: word power. George Carlin's famed Seven Dirty Words were a list related to what you couldn't say on American television in the 1970s: *shit, piss, fuck, cunt, cocksucker, motherfucker,* and *tits.* Now you can say them on cable TV whenever you want—all in a single episode if you so wish. I just wrote a script that has all seven in one scene. But *cunt* still carries a stigma. Even though it's just a word.

Grieve's Fuck Map shows Fuck surrounding the outer edges of America, stretching from the cold beaches of Maine on down the Atlantic seashore, throughout Florida and around the Gulf Coast, along the Mexican border and up the Pacific Coast Highway all the way into Washington State, forming a curse curtain longer and stronger than any wall Trump could ever build. Meanwhile, Cunt gets shunted into the Cunt Corridor of upstate New York and New England. With a dollop of use in Michigan's Upper Peninsula.

We can assume most of these Cunts occur while shoveling snow in 17-degrees-below-zero weather.

Everywhere else in America is basically Cunt-free.

But there is a Cunt Cluster located firmly on the Kentucky-Tennessee border. On the Cunt Map it almost forms a tangerine-colored lipstick kiss. And if you look closely you'll notice that the center of said kiss is the fabulous, party-hardy town of Nashville, truly earning honors as the Cuntry Music Capital of the World. I've been there a few times and let me tell you: they say Cunt so often it makes me feel like I'm back in Dublin. Here's to Nashville for helping Cunt beat Motherfucker in the American Swearing Olympics!

But the rest of the United States has spoken—and Libertards, Conservadicks, and Independent Assholes alike made it clear they do NOT like either word. I think Motherfucker is just having an off season or two and will eventually mount a comeback. But Cunt has been stuck at the bottom of the standings since it was first invented. Cunt is the Cleveland Browns of cursing: a perennial pariah never allowed to rise up the rankings.

Fear not, folks. Dr. Leary may have a solution.

My favorite curse word of all time is one I first heard circa 1973: Goddamncocksuckingmotherlessfuckingcunt.

This was also weather-related. It was uttered by an Irish guy whose car wouldn't start in a Massachusetts nor'easter. And his blizzard of connected curse words pretty much summed up the situation.

Years ago on an episode of *Rescue Me,* Tommy Gavin's soon-to-be ex-wife Janet and current girlfriend Sheila sat in the firehouse kitchen texting insults at each other. Sheila mistypes her final attempt and it beeps into Janet's phone as "CUNF." One letter off. Which is how we got it on TV at the time.

But everyone on the set ended up liking the word so much that we started using it 24/7—in bars, restaurants, offices—any public place we shot in or hung out. It was a blast to see people on the verge of getting upset and outraged, but then holding back because they couldn't be sure whether or not they heard that final *t.*

Now substitute that one letter into the 1973 nor'easter and it still sounds cool: Goddamcocksuckingmotherlessfuckingcunf.

See? It actually adds a nice, soft ending that's a great change of pace from all the *k*'s and *c*'s. Besides, think how awesome it would sound on its own when you tell your boss, "For chris-sakes, Bob, stop being such a cunf."

That welcoming *f* changes everything. It would bring Cunt into the mainstream. It would become a staple in word games and crossword puzzles. For Scrabble alone it'd be a boon. And that new soft sound would make it a hit under any circumstances:

"We stayed at the Cunf Hotel in Cunf, California."

"I had a cunfcake for dessert."

"President Putin is acting far too cunfy on this issue."

Cunf could lead to a revival of Dink—a word that fell out of favor once Dick became popular. But as evidenced by the Grieve study, Dick is no longer a top-ten terror. And as with Cunf, Dink has the agility required for all-access usage, the softer *n* allowing it into locations and conversations that the hard *c* keeps Dick from ever entering. And just like Cunf, Dink's power lies on the tongue of its speaker. The harder you say it, the bigger the hit. But it's not banned. So you could hear Mike Pence say this:

"China is being a real dink when it comes to diplomacy."

To put it in some kind of linguistic equation, Dink is to Cunf as Prick is to Bitch: a complementary curse coupling. And remember, they're all just words. Ever heard of *bint, bellend, minge, spastic,* or *wanker*? In Ireland and the UK you will. And they range from mildly offensive to outright insult. When someone calls you one of them—and they will—don't respond by using the word Cuck. Much to the chagrin of many Trump supporters and cuckservatives, it ain't entering the common idiom. Cuck is not the new Cunt. Cunf is. Call them that and cunfuse them.

Like I said, I'm here to help.

Now that we've discovered some common American ground and hopefully gained enough perspective to see how similar we all really are, let me move forward to help simplify things even further. Forget the Seven Heavenly Virtues and the Seven Deadly Sins—that's fourteen things to keep track of as you go about your very busy day.

And let's be honest here: none of us is capable of being that perfect all the time. Even Jesus snapped at the temple merchants and knocked over their shit while berating their businesses. Right before He cured a bunch of lepers. And made the blind see. But since most of us can't do magic, I'll offer the next best thing: a list.

I'm combining the Virtues with the Sins and giving us a trusty little guide to cover them all. Here's how we handle it at

#ShutTheFuckUpChurch

NEW SEVEN DEADLY SINS, PLUS ONE:
1. Racist? Fuck you.
2. Sexist? Suck balls. 'Cause you sure ain't gettin' any pussy.
3. Misogynist? See above. That's right—you're guilty twice.
4. Lazy asshole? Fuck charity. Until re-binge-watching all five seasons of *Breaking Bad* becomes a job, go get a real one.
5. Drunk or high? Liver transplants are for cancer patients.
6. Selfish prick? Die alone.
7. Fat slob? Try some vanity. Instead of Taco Bell.
8. Stop blaming your parents. You still owe us money.

You may have noticed that in both the Twelve Demandments and the New Seven Deadly Sins, Plus One, the only mention of killing was to enable you to defend yourself. I didn't list murder because we all know it's just unacceptable.

Plus, it takes too much time.

First you have to plan it all in advance, coordinate your schedule with the victim's schedule, pick a place where there won't be any witnesses, and then map out approach and escape routes. But even if it's a sudden crime of passion, you still have to clean afterward. For hours on end.

Walls and floors need to be wiped down and mopped up. Fingerprints have to be buffed off of doorknobs and kitchen utensils. Even if you wear gloves, you have to worry about fabric fibers and blood smudges.

This is even before driving the body someplace to dispose of it, unless you plan on cutting it up—and THAT'S a mess you'll be spending all night on—not to mention having to buy industrial-strength garbage bags, large gallons of disinfectant, and a selection of small power saws. And you'll probably have to do laundry, too. Or find an incinerator. Or burn your pants, shirt, and shoes in the woods somewhere. Which involves even MORE driving. And a change of clothes.

No wonder they pay hit men so much money.

This is where good old-fashioned revenge comes in. Sure it may take longer. But revenge is sweet—and highly underrated.

I have this thing that happens to me whenever I hate somebody: their name disappears from my memory bank. This happened even when I was in my thirties and not worried about early-onset Alzheimer's or the faded edges of the aging process. If you fucked me over, my brain erased your name. I could remember your face, but I'd have to ask a friend or coworker, "What the hell was the name of that guy we hated who used to be at HBO?"

But deep in the forested Irish recesses of my gray matter is a lush green clearing where I can always find My Top Five Enemies of All Time. Selfish evil assholes I came across early in life who screwed me and my friends over in so deliberate and criminal a fashion that I'm still waiting for each one to die a long, horrible, and early fucking death.

I don't nurse my grudges. I juice them with steroids and keep them in cage-fighting shape.

The late great Carrie Fisher once said something I'll never forget: "Revenge is like drinking poison and waiting for the other person to die."

And that may be true.

But in the case of these guys, it's not a daily venomous bile that restricts my ability to enjoy life. It's not even a weekly dose of noxious air that momentarily shuts down my operating system.

It's just a latent desire to celebrate if the news arrives that one of them has been smote by karma.

Or cancer.

Or a bus.

'Cause that's what gets me in this God business: karma. Too often in my life I've seen great men and women wiped off the planet long before their time. Unselfish, truly talented, and caring people who looked out for others and loved their families and friends. Firefighters and film directors. Schoolteachers and soldiers. Or just your average American living a life full of hard work and honest hours.

The guys on my grudge list each spend their days stealing money from the sweat and elbow grease of others, and show no remorse for their crimes. They attached themselves to the American way at an early age like a parasitic tick just sucking up what they needed with no regard for anyone else.

I know it's an ancient question, but when a great guy like my firefighter cousin Jerry Lucey gives his life in an empty warehouse blaze to save some homeless people, yet the selfish, piece-of-shit junkie who started that fire still walks the streets? I gotta wonder where God is and what the fuck His master plan contains.

And I know that sometimes evil, empty souls can suddenly see the light and turn their lives around—pull a one-eighty and start doing good instead of bad. This usually involves a medical scare.

One guy on my list is a fifty-eight-year-old cokeheaded asshole who's done nothing except mooch his way through the last five decades. Stole cash when he couldn't borrow it. Ripped off people who worked for him. Never a red cent spent on anyone else. Family hates him. Never talks to his ex-wife or kids. Total waste.

Then last year he had a massive stroke. Lost the use of his left arm and the sight in one eye. He was in the hospital clinging to life for a few days. And I'm not ashamed to admit that several friends of mine were hoping he wouldn't make it.

As was I.

Guess what? He DID make it. And you know what he is now? A one-armed, half-blind, cokeheaded asshole. So forgive me if I dance on his grave once it gets dug.

I did figuratively dance on the graves of two other scumbags who I'm glad to say no longer suck anyone's blood or money.

One guy woke up dead. Which is a shame. I would have preferred some pain, maybe a stroke or two—at least an elongated heart attack where he had to fight for breath.

Instead?

He died in his sleep after ingesting nine OxyContins and a bottle of peppermint schnapps. Which gives you some idea of how he spent his days on earth: in a stupor. After dragging his aging parents through six rounds of rehab and countless arrests, not to mention a few hundred thousand of their hard-earned dollars.

When the call came in from a mutual friend, the only grieving we did was for his mom and dad, and even that was actually just a sad form of relief. This guy was such a nasty piece of work that even his current girlfriend refused to come to the funeral. Only eight people showed up. One was his probation officer. Probably to make sure it wasn't just another scam. If I had my way, his tombstone would read GOOD RIDDANCE.

During the phone calls celebrating this fuckbucket's demise, two of my oldest friends brought up another cockwomble who hadn't come close to an early death yet. Matter of fact, he was walking through the new millennium healthy as a horse: no cancer, no liver failure, no arrest record—nothing. He was actually thriving. After years of running nightclubs and concert venues from which he robbed bands, comedians, waitstaff, and bouncers blind—after not paying taxes on barrels full of other people's cash—this jizztrumpet was living the life in a nice beach house full of bad vibes and high-end escort chicks. He'd learned how to beat the system, but the one trick he never picked up?

How to swim drunk.

They found his body the day after a late-night skinny-dip and man, did the phone calls fly. I'm talking multiple calls from musicians, comics, and other club owners celebrating this douchecanoe's demise.

A mere eight months after the first asshole.

Do I feel a twinge of guilt or some hint of remorse about getting such joy from another human being's misfortune? Let me put it this way: two down, three to go.

Yeah, revenge IS like drinking poison and waiting for the other person to die. But sometimes they die first. And take it from someone who knows: it feels FUCKING AWESOME!

Maybe there is a God after all.

And Her name is Princess Leia.

Fame changes a lot of things. But it can't change a light bulb.

—GILDA RADNER

SOCIAL MEDIA DISEASE

Last summer, Katy Perry streamed ninety-six pure, unfiltered hours of her life online—every inch, every ounce of her daily details and dilemmas. For four whole uninterrupted days you could watch Katy sleep, eat, cry, whine, curse, drink, and slather on makeup. And tell her shrink she's addicted to attention. Which she got from an estimated forty million sets of eyeballs. Who sent out ninety-six hours of tweets, Snapchats, and Instagrams about it.

This is what happens when you put smartphones into the hands of Stupidfuckingpeople.

Scientists once believed that instant handheld access to all available information would make us more intelligent and aware of the world we live in. Help us to open constructive conversation with all the other inhabitants of planet earth. Globally it has been a vital tool for fighting against injustice, hunger, and war crimes. So what are we Americans using it for?

To chime in on Katy's beef with Taylor Swift. About stolen backup dancers.

And to send twitpics of our cupcakes. Not to mention cocktails, pie, and pasta.

If you follow me on social media you may have noticed that I don't take pictures of my food. Why? Because I'm too busy fucking eating it. But I did chime in on Twitter about how we could end the Perry–Swift War. Make them both listen to an Aretha Franklin song and suddenly realize—*holy shit: we suck.*

Katy didn't take my advice. But she did take the time to extend this peace offering to Taylor: "I think we can be like, you know, representatives of strong women that come together despite their differences, then like the whole world is going to go, like, 'Yeah, we can do this!' "

If only Israel and Palestine were arguing about backup dancers. Or ISIS hated us because of our choreography. Then "Katy 2020" could become a rallying cry!

#KissedAJewAndLikedIt #CherryHebrewChapstick

By the way, during her promotional self-a-thon, Katy tweeted out pics, gifs, and memes of all her meals. This shit is becoming an irreversible virus.

Even our new leader can't stop his tiny digits from tweeting about Trump Tower tacos and Kentucky Fried Chicken. Not to mention any instant idea that pops into his OCD head just as fast as he can type. Which may explain his rediculous, dum, and unpresidented spelling mistakes.

His Twitter feed is full of such unchecked English, along with reams of humblebrags and arrogant blame placement. Can you imagine if past world leaders had access to this kind of technology? I did. When Trump visited the site of Lincoln's hallowed Gettysburg Address on a campaign stop, I listened to his speech and couldn't stop laughing.

In the midst of a terrifying civil war rooted in the battle to abolish slavery, Lincoln had spoken of "a new nation, conceived in Liberty and dedicated to the proposition that all men are created equal." Trump's speech on the same sacred site was rightly nicknamed the Grievanceburg Address as he threatened civil lawsuits toward eleven women who had accused him of sexual assault.

Lincoln's speech lasted two minutes.

Trump's? Forty-one minutes and fifty-five seconds. After which he tweeted six times.

On February 2, 2017, the National Archives and Record Administration announced that all of Trump's tweets would need to be saved because the Presidential Records Act now reaches into the social media activity of any POTUS, including any deleted tweets. Which means this all-time Trump favorite of mine will be saved there—and here—for posterity:

DONALD J. TRUMP
@realDonaldTrump

`Following`

I would like to extend my best wishes to all, even the haters and losers, on this special date, September 11th.

RETWEETS	LIKES	
4,510	**4,138**	

7:21 AM - 11 Sep 2013

Imagine if world leaders throughout history expressed themselves with such infantile, braggadocious abandon? Here are some choice social media moments from previous centuries, as delivered by noted figures if—like Trump—they just couldn't fight the urge to instantly express each inane thought tickling their itchy little brains. I call it:

FOUR SCORE AND 7 SECONDS AGO

THOMAS JEFFERSON
@3rdPOTUS

`Following`

Writer, farmer, statesman. Virginia is for lovers.

What happens in the Big House stays in the Big House. #OnceYouGoSlave

RETWEETS	LIKES	
1,175	**25K**	

3:45 AM - 4 Jun 1803

DOLLEY MADISON
@4thFLOTUS

You're looking swell, Dolley.

James thinks it would be okay to sell my cakes and pies on the side. How about reading the Constitution, dipshit?

RETWEETS   LIKES
5   27

4:32 AM - 11 Feb 1813

ABRAHAM LINCOLN
@HonestPOTUS

16th President, 2nd marriage, guy on the 5.

Failing @GettysburgGazette forgot to publish last 2/3 of my address to troops, plus song parody. Hacks!

RETWEETS   LIKES
26K   57K

5:02 AM - 22 Nov 1863

ULYSSES S. GRANT
@FuturePOTUS

Following

War Hero, Husband, Not a Fucking Drunk.

Dear @robertelee: terms of surrender include changing your name to Lou Zer & sucking our dix. Sie? #BringBourbon

RETWEETS LIKES
2.2 M 525,779

4:11 AM - 8 Apr 1865

ABRAHAM LINCOLN
@HonestPOTUS

Following

16th President, 2nd marriage, guy on the 5.

Let me get this straight: I freed the slaves but I can't get out of going to the theater? #KillMe #GonnaHitTheStovePipe

RETWEETS LIKES
659 3,556

5:56 PM - 15 Apr 1865

THEODORE ROOSEVELT Following
@TeddyPOTUS

Rough Rider, Asthma Sufferer. No smokers.

Ladies, when I say I carry a big stick, it's not a euphemism, believe me. #MakeAmericaBullyAgain

RETWEETS   LIKES
668   1,207

4:46 AM - 15 Sep 1901

GEORGE S. PATTON Following
@CowardKiller

Invented the tank. And balls. Which won us WW1.

Excuse my French but these fucking Krauts, Chinks & Wops will start another war. Probly cause they hate the goddam Kikes.

RETWEETS   LIKES
7   47,891

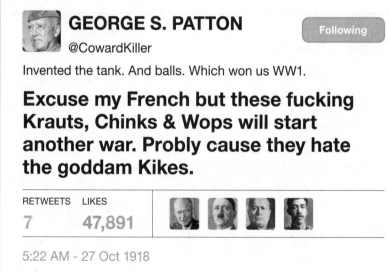

5:22 AM - 27 Oct 1918

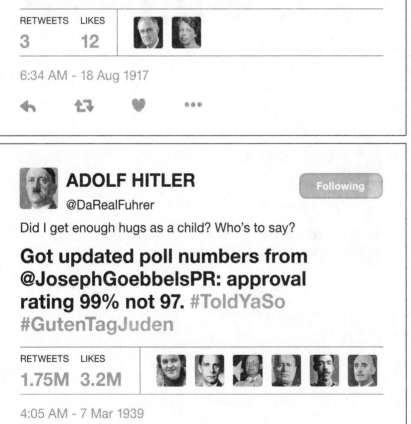

THEODORE ROOSEVELT
@TeddyPOTUS
Following

Exprez. Explorer.

#HolyShit **Just drove thru South Dakota. Saw a mountain that looked like me. Gotta cut back on the cough syrup.**

RETWEETS | LIKES
3 | 12

6:34 AM - 18 Aug 1917

ADOLF HITLER
@DaRealFuhrer
Following

Did I get enough hugs as a child? Who's to say?

Got updated poll numbers from @JosephGoebbelsPR: approval rating 99% not 97. #ToldYaSo #GutenTagJuden

RETWEETS | LIKES
1.75M | 3.2M

4:05 AM - 7 Mar 1939

ELEANOR ROOSEVELT

@FirstBroadOne

Behind every great man—a woman pushing the chair.

FYI the next guy who asks me if I need my husband's braces is gonna need the Red Fucking Cross!

RETWEETS	LIKES
1.3M	2.6M

5:23 AM - 17 Feb 1940

EVA BRAUN
@MrsHitler?

Former photographer, future bride.

Last time I blow @HermannGoering without getting the morphine up front.

RETWEETS	LIKES
1	4

4:51 AM - 15 Mar 1940

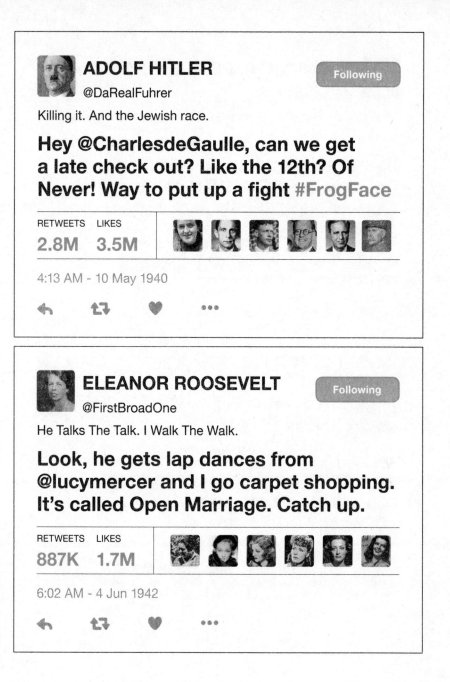

ADOLF HITLER
@DaRealFuhrer

Following

Killing it. And the Jewish race.

Hey @CharlesdeGaulle, can we get a late check out? Like the 12th? Of Never! Way to put up a fight #FrogFace

RETWEETS | LIKES
2.8M | 3.5M

4:13 AM - 10 May 1940

ELEANOR ROOSEVELT
@FirstBroadOne

Following

He Talks The Talk. I Walk The Walk.

Look, he gets lap dances from @lucymercer and I go carpet shopping. It's called Open Marriage. Catch up.

RETWEETS | LIKES
887K | 1.7M

6:02 AM - 4 Jun 1942

FRANKLIN D. ROOSEVELT Following

@FDfuckinR

Ended Great Depression, Won WW2. What'd you do today, Gladys?

Fourth term motherfuckers! Packing the SCOTUS with cripples! #BenevolentDictator #ChairForce

RETWEETS	LIKES	
2.3M	3.6M	

5:01 AM - 5 Mar 1945

 EVA BRAUN Following

@MrsHitler

Winner of 1945 Berlin Bridal Gown Award.

Anyone know if it's okay to take cyanide capsules on an empty stomach?

RETWEETS	LIKES	
27M	6M	

6:37 AM - 29 Apr 1945

HARRY S. TRUMAN

Following

@GiveEmHellPOTUS

Proud Missourian, Bess Boy.

Hey @Tojo: funny, you don't look Enola Gay. Soup of the day? #MushroomCloud

RETWEETS	LIKES	
5.4M	7.3M	

4:38 AM - 6 Aug 1945

DWIGHT D. EISENHOWER

Following

@5StarPOTUS

Brilliant Military Tactician, Shitty Putter, Honorary Bald Eagle.

Dear @GeneralDouglasMacArthur: you still mad, bro?

RETWEETS	LIKES	
18,327	33,432	

6:01 AM - 21 Jan 1953

PAT NIXON
@MissesDick

Cloth Coat Club. Not an accomplice.

Having trouble with @WhiteHouse phones. When I'm talking to Tricia it sounds like there's someone else on the line, eating.

RETWEETS	LIKES	
1	8	

7:24 AM - 8 Feb 1973

GOLDA MEIR
@SolidGolda

Prime Minister, Stateswoman, Former Hand Model.

If @MosheDayan says to me "Hey Jake when's your next fight?" one more time—no shit, the other eye goes.

RETWEETS	LIKES	
265	347	

4:17 AM - 28 Jul 1973

PAT NIXON

@MissesDick

Former First Lady. Current bitter spouse.

Just found out wife can't testify against husband. Bad!

RETWEETS	LIKES
2	12

5:47 AM - 31 Aug 1974

BETTY FORD

@GerrysBitch

Disco doesn't suck, Jimmy Carter does.

So he keeps falling down but I have to go to rehab. #DoubleFuckingStandard

RETWEETS	LIKES
37	672

4:25 AM - 14 Nov 1975

MARGARET TRUDEAU

Following

@wakeupmaggie

Estranged First Lady of Canada. Studio 54 VIP.

Difference between the Mahovlich brothers? When Frank goes down on you he takes his teeth out.

RETWEETS LIKES

87   176

3:35 PM - 28 May 1976

IDI AMIN

Following

@hallelujahamin

Ugandan Strongman, Recovering Genocider, Polygamist, Pisces.

New year's resolution: start eating healthier. Only gluten-free people.

RETWEETS LIKES

1.7M   3.1M

4:43 AM - 1 Jan 1977

BETTY FORD

@GerrysBitch

Following

Rosalynn Carter is a cunt.

That was not a typo in @GoodHousekeeping, my rice pudding recipe calls for 7 bottles of vanilla extract. #LickMe

RETWEETS LIKES

103   542

6:39 AM - 25 Dec 1977

NANCY REAGAN

@Mommy1

Following

Playing the role of Jane Wyman—forever!

Blew entire AIDS budget for 1985. Just Say No to astrologers who think they can play the horses.

RETWEETS LIKES

4,389 12,786

3:57 AM - 21 Oct 1985

GEORGE H. W. BUSH
@ReadMyLips

40th & 41st POTUS. Oh, like I didn't run the country after Reagan got shot.

Me & @JebBush still laughing about George Jr. saying he's gonna b Prez one day #OldestChildSyndrome #LayOffTheSnow

RETWEETS	LIKES	
2,317	4,521	

11:37 PM - 27 Jan 1989

 SADDAM HUSSEIN
@husseiniac

Tortured soul . . . and 200,000 dissidents.

Sunday @ThePalace 12-2 pm First Annual Mustard Gas Cook-Off! 1st Prize: oil field in Fallujah. 2nd: oil field in Kuwait.

RETWEETS	LIKES	
879	5,499	

4:10 AM - 14 July 1990

If only.

What a trip they all would have been on Twitter. Each one is now forever famous for great achievements or eternally infamous for failed events and ideas.

But the key part of the formula usually is this: most presidents and world leaders gain their biggest audience AFTER they begin their public bid for power. The campaign trail is the fame highway that transforms them into a household name.

Not The Donald.

Trump had thirty million followers before he even thought of running for the Oval Office. Because he was already a celebrity. And these days it seems everyone in America wants to be associated with one. Or become a celebrity themselves. As a matter of fact, many were more likely to follow Trump on Twitter than to actually vote for him.

Out of the 240 million Americans eligible to vote in the last election, over 100 million never even bothered to show up. They could care less about politics. One poll showed that more of us were concerned about losing belly fat than what Trump or Hillary might do to the country. It's been this way for decades now, but in the last eight years such apathy has reached supersonic levels.

To the point of parody.

One day in February 2016, 439,102 people voted in Kim Kardashian's Twitter poll asking fans to name her husband Kanye West's new album. That same day, only 135,077 people voted in the GOP presidential caucus.

I guess it makes sense. And could be another form of thinning the herd. Do we really want reality TV fans voting for president? Too late—they already did. One pre-2016 election poll showed that most Americans knew Trump as a television host, not as an actual businessman. They loved his brash behavior and coldhearted "You're fired!" catchphrase. And his hair. They looooved staring at his hair. It currently has five Twitter accounts. And there are another four dedicated only to his hands.

This is our future, folks. Where shucking your shame, blame, face, and body on a daily digital or weekly televised basis is now a career option. Forget the Me Generation. This is Me Me Me 24/7/365. Like me on this, love me on that. My hair, my face, my media, my memes.

And our taste runs to social media accounts belonging to self-involved celebs. The top five Twitter feeds in the world?

@katyperry	96 million
@justinbieber	93 million
@barackobama	89 million
@taylorswift13	84 million
@rihanna	70 million

@YouTube came in a distant sixth. I'd say it's the only actual entity on the list, but every single person in the top five is an entity. Operating on a higher plane than the rest of us. Not just a celebrity, but celebrated and elevated.

The only world leader in that group is President Obama. Who has tweeted 15,000 times in ten years—mostly about hope and change and why it still might happen. Sounds like a lot until you find out our current president has tweeted over 35,000 times in eight years, an average of fourteen times a day.

And always about himself.

Which is what Katy Perry does. And Bieber. And Swift and Ri-hanna and every other major pop star. But they ain't occupying the Oval Office. Although they might as well be. Because people flock to these feeds like it's a life force that can save a hungry human soul. Not famous themselves but somehow adjacent to fame. As if that will eventually gain them a touch of notoriety too.

People stand outside the glass windows of every New York City morning show studio, waving like fools and using selfie sticks to immortalize their time as human stick figures on deep-background TV. Then send the pics soaring out into the anony-mous social media stratosphere hoping to get some kind of hits that say I SEE YOU! WISH I WERE YOU! CUTE JEANS!, but mostly become FUCK YOU! FAT ASS! DUMB CUNT! So they spend another few hours feuding back and forth in 140 charac-ters or less.

I don't do Twitter feuds. I prefer a good, old-fashioned, face-to-face *Fuck you.*

If you don't want Twitter trolls making comments about how fat your ass is, here's a very simple solution: stop posting pic-tures of it. Besides, most of these idiots cutting you down have 7,000 tweets and six followers. Heads up, half-wits: Jesus was a pariah in his own time and he had twelve.

By the way, you want to know how you stop a cyberbully? Pay at-tention now, because the answer is a little complicated. Ready? Here it is:

TURN OFF YOUR FUCKING PHONE!

Read something other than your own social media apps. Buy a fucking book. And for God's sake stop taking selfies every fifteen seconds.

Twenty-four billion selfies were uploaded to Google Photos last year. Twenty-one billion of them with some form of face-slimming filter. That's supposed to be a joke but instead sounds like a real possibility, doesn't it? The amount of time spent photographing ourselves and then altering the images is astounding. And sometimes fatal.

There are now actual stats on selfie-related deaths—called "killfies"—when people die while trying visual stunts to gain some social media magnificence. In 2014, fifteen people died this way. In 2015, it was thirty-nine. Last year, seventy-three people met the grim reaper while pointing their phones at their faces in dangerous places, and this year's number is predicted to finish somewhere north of 150.

So far in 2017:

Two teens taking a selfie on the tarmac were killed by a landing airplane.

A kid seeking a bigger Snapchat audience had his girlfriend film him as he parkoured onto a third-floor mall railing. Only problem? He missed. And fell to his mushy death.

One college released a statement concerning the death of a student who was live-streaming himself as he tried to chug ten mai tais in less than two minutes. It might as well have read: THIS WAS A TEST.

You read that right. Tragic? Yeah. Stupid? FUCK yeah. But I say these addlepated idiots are doing humanity a favor. They are thinning the herd FOR us. Here's the official list based on a recent university-sponsored data study:

FREQUENCY OF SELFIE-RELATED DEATHS, 2010–2017
1. Falling from Great Heights While Posing
2. Falling from Great Heights into the Ocean While Posing
3. Posing On, Near, or In Front of Trains
4. Drowning While Posing (boats, logs, surfboards)
5. Accidental Shooting While Posing with a Gun
6. Hit by Truck, Bus, or Car While Posing
7. Poisonous Bite While Posing with a Rattlesnake
8. Bison
9. Grenades
10. Juggling (fire, knives, chainsaws, and chainsaws on fire)

Are we really going to miss any of these asinine dopes? No. We shouldn't be warning them. We should be encouraging them. If you're enough of a fatuous pinhead to have your death make this list, you deserve to disappear. Posing with a rattlesnake? Sorry, that's not just a grave error. It's a way to find and eliminate jackasses.

And as bad as the first seven are, the last three don't even mention posing on, near, or with the cause of death. Which implies what? Taunting a bison? Tossing a grenade? Again, if this is how some lummox plans to get famous, don't stop him. Instead? Hand that goon a grenade. They wanna fuck with a bison? Let's open a Bison Amusement Park and make some cash off these clods.

Better yet, let's combine it all together. I'm sure there is some chump out there who wants to ride a bison while juggling grenades AND his cell phone—live on Snapchat. What I wouldn't give to see THAT motherfucker die.

And therein lies the real problem with all of this. It's not the dullards who hatch these dense ideas. It's us—the audience who watches their stupefying torpidity. The dumber they are, the more superior we feel.

Each one of these oafs wanted to go viral. And you can bet your left nut that—had they survived—their injury-inducing selfies would have sucked in an almost endless supply of putdowns and negative posts. Nothing brings out the insults and online abuse more than a bunch of mutton-headed Darwin Award winners who are self-chlorinating the gene pool. We can only look good by comparison.

As we say in Boston: it makes us feel wicked smahht.

That's why we all love reality TV. The more puerile and scummy the dolts on these shows get, the more self-esteem we accumulate by watching them. And my, how the ratings rise.

Each week, our eyes and ears get assaulted by the overheated mewling of supposed Real Housewives whose only desire is to be so outrageously memorable that they can tie their tawdry names to clothing, booze, and food products.

I never set out to watch these shows, but having walked in on countless friends and family members doing so during the first season of *Real Housewives of New York City,* I couldn't figure out why.

Until I gazed at a few minutes of it. Holy shit. The fighting and feuding. The insults and alcohol flying back and forth. The narrow-minded emotional minutiae and flat-out egotistical fury of it all. Half an hour in? I felt like a saint. Like Mother Fucking Theresa. Like I was such a good person I should be nominated for a Nobel Prize.

And the biggest surprise of all was Bethenny Frankel.

Bethenny used to work for me as the set chef on *Rescue Me*. She was funny and fast and an amazing cook. Seeing her on that show was like doing a fame double-take. She wasn't only the brightest person in the cast, she was suddenly a bigger star than I'll ever be.

I was pretty much done with it after a couple of viewings. But that's when I came to realize there was no escape.

Like all of us, I've had the horror of seeing the endless promos packed with their latest season-ending, shriek-filled, ear-bleeding tirades. And felt their Botoxed eyeballs and trout-pout lips leaping out at me from a zillion magazine displays. We can't escape their vacant stares or overinflated balloon tits.

Or the millions of other needy fuckwads constantly clawing their way up the ladder of public performance. It's a nonstop cry for attention by people who are famous for doing nothing other than exposing their surgically altered asses all over every available electronic device you own.

YouTube talents and Instagram stars. Facebook virtuosos and Snapchat VIPs. Who would all kill to get on reality TV. Where the crowded field is already packed with ego-deranged fools. Singers, actors, and ex-athletes. Girlfriends, husbands, wives, and ex-wives. Real estate brokers and construction workers. People who hunt, pawn, pour, paint, drive, fix, and fish for a living—all aiming to become household names, to join what they see as the rich and rarefied celebrity class, where their actions, quotes, and looks can be paid for and adored. Every single one of them dying to be famous in the worst way.

Which is usually how they end up achieving it.

Because no one thinks about the consequences. Where once you make a name for yourself, each and every embarrassing drunken foible or drug-induced mistake is covered as breaking news on Twitter and TMZ.

Let's put the chase for fame into some form of reasonable perspective. The next time you think you're one in a million, placed on this crowded earth because your outstanding talent, unique looks, and incredibly witty remarks deserve to be noticed and publicly acknowledged—and that somehow luck or divine intervention will lead you to the golden corridors of Hollywood's promised land—take a beat.

Then visit a site called InternetLiveStats.com. I did so at 7:36 a.m. on March 31, 2017, and here's what was happening:

CURRENT USERS OF INTERNET: 3,600,883,045
CURRENT TWEETS SENT TODAY: 207,149,787
CURRENT INSTAGRAM PHOTOS POSTED TODAY:
    21,209,631
CURRENT BLOG POSTS WRITTEN TODAY: 1,522,608
CURRENT FACEBOOK ACTIVE USERS: 1,878,623,995

There are 430,000 tweets per minute in America, 500 million tweets every twenty-four hours.

All day. Every day. An endless ocean of anonymity. Reminding us all: we ain't nothin' special.

Nanosecond after millisecond, fake faces and real food and snarky remarks and their angry ranting replies—tits, pecs, postures, and posteriors fly into and out of our cell phones, singeing the retinas with vapid information. Everybody screaming to be seen and heard.

I've been a celebrity for exactly twenty-five years now. Seen it from every angle. Clacking up to the tippity top and then speeding straight down the insane fame roller coaster—the rush of it all sucking the air from your lungs. And the whole 1,000-mile-per-hour rocket ship trip done without any brakes. Hair blown back, stomach in your throat, best-laid plans flying out of your hands and fluttering away in the wind.

The term "overnight sensation" isn't technically true. It takes quite a while to happen, but once your recognition starts to pop, it does feel like you wake up one morning and your world has been altered. Suddenly everyone knows who you are. People stare and point and shout your name. And everyone wants a piece of you. And to many old friends—as well as many new ones—you become a human dollar sign.

I'm not complaining: fame and success brought wealth and security for my wife and kids and many members of our extended family. And you do find out who your real friends are—or should I say WERE—very, very quickly.

If you're a comedian, old friends from your club days suddenly accuse you of stealing ideas. Or subjects. As if Lenny Bruce, Richard Pryor, George Carlin, and Joan Rivers hadn't already covered every topic known to stand-up. But once you make it big, these old pals can turn into newfound enemies. As they gander at you on Conan or Fallon, they see ghosts of their own jokes in every word you utter. The funnier and more famous you get, the more furious and ridiculous the charges. I once had a close comedy compadre accuse me of stealing one of his hand gestures. I repeat: a hand gesture. Said he saw me make it during an appearance on Letterman, which he watched three times. Once in slow motion. He also thought Letterman stole one of his jokes. That's how deeply fame can infect the non-famous.

A rock 'n' roll lead singer pal of mine was accused of stealing a stage pose by a far less successful singer, who saw him strike it on Jimmy Kimmel. This guy claimed he'd invented the pose. When my pal said he saw David Bowie do the same move back in the early nineties, the accuser said, "Yeah, but I made it better."

In the recording business, famous bands are often hit with allegations of lifting a riff, looting a look, or adopting a "vibe"— always by bands that never made it.

A famous actor pal of mine once got rave reviews for his Richard III and then faced allegations of theft from one of his old acting school classmates, who said my pal had stolen his "cadence." It seems that when this guy saw my friend's performance, all he could hear was his own voice. Which was not a famous one.

In all three branches of showbiz, former friends who don't make it as far will curse your fame with a series of bitter salvos aimed at everyone except themselves, or claim the only difference between your success and their failure is this: you just got lucky.

And luck is a part of it all. Luck matters. Ask any famous person and they'll have a comment or two on the role happenstance played in their careers. Here are some great quotes on the subject from some very noteworthy people:

Success is simply a matter of luck. Just ask any failure.
—Earl Wilson

When it comes to luck, you make your own.
—Bruce Springsteen

The harder I work, the luckier I get.
—Sam Goldwyn

**I do believe in luck. How else can I explain the success
of all the fucking assholes I hate?**
—My Friend Fitzy

Okay, Fitzy's not famous. But he does sum up how a lot of jealous people approach the accomplishments of others: it's easier for them to justify their own misfortune by pointing at your success and saying you don't deserve it. Behind every famous athlete, comic, actor, singer, writer, and politician you are aware of, there are fifteen people you've never heard about saying "that should have been me."

Shoulda, woulda, coulda. Each famous person I've ever gotten to know tells a tale of ex-friends lost on the trail of bitter showbiz tears. They can't see the mountain for your trees.

How many humans actually have the balls to look in the mirror and blame themselves for failing to make it? Answer: not enough.

Trump never points the finger at himself for either his very public business fuckups as a private citizen or his even more public mistakes and blunders as president. Love him or hate him, he did win the election and Hillary's probably still blaming Bill for that. Bernie's busy blaming both of them and Donna Brazile. As JFK once said: victory has a thousand fathers and defeat is an orphan.

Nobody wants to shoulder the blame for their own demise.

Few and far between are those public figures willing to stand up and take the beating when things don't go the way they planned. Or even accept the facts when it comes to their own lack of ability.

Whitey Herzog was a Hall of Fame baseball manager known for speaking his mind. After taking the reins of the last-place Texas Rangers in the fall of 1972, he told reporters, "If Rich Billings is our starting catcher again next year, this club is in deep trouble." To which Billings later replied: "He's obviously seen me play."

Wouldn't it be nice if more famous people had the same sense of humor and honesty when it came to facing their limitations?

I'll give you just one glaring example of when mine came into undeniable focus: watching *The Amazing Spiderman* in 3D. I knew my nose was big. I'm not a moron. I've lived with the thing for six fucking decades. But it's one thing to see it in a mirror and a whole different nightmare to see it on the big screen wearing 3D glasses. With a thousand people watching. My kids wanted to attend the splashy L.A. premiere of the movie—they begged and pleaded, so off we went.

Now this may sound strange, but if I'm not producing or directing something I'm in, I don't watch it the way you do. When I'm involved in the process of editing and mixing, I can be objective about my own performance and judge it purely as part of the overall story. But if I'm just acting in a movie, watching it fills me with remorse about other creative choices I could have made, what I could have done better. I'm not looking at myself in terms of appearance. I'm looking at the character.

But seeing Captain Stacy's nose in three-dimensional display four stories high? That nose didn't belong to him—it was all mine. The thing was massive. You could have parked four school buses inside each nostril. And the school.

About four seconds after I first showed up on the giant screen, I tore off the 3D glasses. Thirty seconds later I was out in the lobby having a smoke and making an early entrance to the after-party. With what now felt like a much smaller snout.

A little bit of humility can be very useful out on the public stage. And hard work. That's the real difference between being a flash in the pan or a perennial presence. Today's headlines or yesterday's news. There are boatloads of gifted people on this planet, no matter what field you wish to compete in. But are you willing to make the sacrifice and put in the effort it takes to excel?

Hall of Fame hoop star Larry Bird took three hundred practice shots before every single game he ever played. Fifty-plus years into their career, The Rolling Stones still rehearse for a minimum of four weeks before heading out on each tour. Pulitzer Prize–winning historian Robert Caro's first book about LBJ took six years to research and write. The second one took eight years. The third? Twelve.

Lady Gaga burst onto the music scene like a lightning rod in 2008, only twenty-two years old at the time. Her first two singles shot through pop culture. Many critics considered her a two-hit wonder. After she wore a dress made of raw meat to the 2010 MTV Music Video Awards, several of them wrote her off as an attention-seeking gimmick machine.

Seven years later they are still wrong.

And it's not because she continues to show up on the red carpet wearing a see-through plastic bubble and boots made out of dwarves. It's because she spends countless hours writing and creating original music and puts on a three-hour live show full of acrobatic dance moves and furious vocal maneuvers without one single note of lip-synching.

She's the Real Fucking Deal.

And of course she's been accused by musician friends from the old days and various no-name bands of stealing ideas, riffs, her persona, and—believe it or not—even the meat dress.

Every time you see someone like Gaga blowing the lid off an awards show with an amazing performance, there's bound to be a bitter bunch of unknown artists she started out with tossing back beers and bemoaning her existence. Instead of getting on with their own careers. Or switching careers because they just don't have what it takes to make it.

Like Gaga once said: she was famous before we knew who she was. Celebrating her own private celebrity. A star in her own life. Walking the same walk, talking the same talk. Without money or a trail of paparazzi. For some people, being famous in their own lives should not only be enough, it's probably even better.

I have a friend who was a star hockey player in high school and thought he'd end up playing in the National Hockey League. He was by far the best center in the state where he was raised—a natural scoring machine. Not much of a defensive player, but hey, when you're putting the puck in the net two times a game, nobody complains about your back-checking. He didn't have to try harder, he was born better.

And got drafted in the first round.

The second best player from his school didn't get drafted at all. He was too small, too slow, and not a natural scorer.

Within three years, my buddy was out of the game, blaming his coaches and the shitty minor league teams he played on for ruining his career. His excuses? They never gave him a chance to shine, didn't know how to get him the puck, wouldn't let him play his game, blah blubbedy blah.

So he moved back home and became a firefighter. A great fire-fighter. Highly decorated. Respected and trusted by his crew.

The second best player? He was a walk-on at an NHL camp. Made the cut. Worked his ass off in the minors. Listened to the coaching staff when they taught him new techniques. Became an all-around player who hustled his balls off and never complained. His professional career lasted for ten years.

My buddy never stopped grumbling about that. Every time we saw the second best player skating in a big tilt on TV, or in an article in the paper about his hustle and grit, my friend would rant and rave about how much better HE could have been if he'd only been able to do it all his way.

"I got fuckin' screwed!" became his mantra.

Until one night when he was bitching about his nemesis so much that a fellow firefighter finally said, "Dude, there are three people walking around this city tonight because you personally saved their lives during a fire last year. Not to mention about six other people you saved during the last two decades. Fuck hockey. You were born to do THIS job. You didn't get screwed. You got pointed in the right direction."

And that was the moment he gave up the ghost. From that simple statement on, he's been a satisfied guy. In a perfect world he WOULD be famous. For running into burning buildings when everyone else is running out.

The celebrity spotlight ain't for everyone. People think it's a magic wand that will solve all their problems—financially and emotionally. Having been exposed to the hot white light of Hollywood for two and a half decades, I can tell you this: fame isn't a cure for anything. Matter of fact, fame is the disease.

And it's eating our country alive.

A few years back, the Wagner Group conducted their first-ever poll to determine the 100 Most Trusted People in America—deep research on multiple levels testing several different layers of confidence, reliability, and faith in public figures. Here's the top ten, plus one:

1. Tom Hanks
2. Sandra Bullock
3. Denzel Washington
4. Meryl Streep
5. Maya Angelou
6. Steven Spielberg
7. Bill Gates
8. Alex Trebek
9. Melinda Gates
10. Julia Roberts
11. Dr. Robert Lefkowitz

Now there are several shocking things to discuss here. First and most obvious: Sandra Bullock is number two? In my book she's number one. She and I go way back to when we were both just starting out—we did *Demolition Man* and *Two If by Sea* together, so I may be biased, but you know what?

Fuck it.

I am biased.

I don't know Tom Hanks. But I know you could hand your car keys to Sandra Bullock and say go pick up two cases of beer and some vodka and she would not only do it no questions asked, she'd be back in a flash. At least in the old days. Would Tom Hanks do that? He looks like the kind of guy who wouldn't. He seems like he would try to talk you out of partying and hold onto your keys in case you drank too much.

Which, come to think of it, is probably why he's number one. Okay, I get it now. He stays.

The second most obvious shocker? That I came in at number fifty-seven. I'm kidding. I wasn't number fifty-seven.

I was ninety-four!

Sorry. Totally fucking with you now. I'm not on the list. Or probably even anywhere in the top thousand. And I shouldn't be. Neither should Sandy or Tom. Or Denzel. No actors should be. Never mind five actors in the first ten spots. And if that isn't bad enough, Alex Trebek at number eight? Seriously? He doesn't actually know the answers to the questions, folks—he's just really, really good at reading them off of index cards. And he's a Canadian. Who doesn't fucking skate anymore. Which would put him even higher than eight on the 100 Least Trusted Canadians list.

The real shocker in this poll, though, is number eleven: Dr. Robert Lefkowitz. Not because he's the only doctor on the list and should have finished even higher, but I'm shocked that people actually know who the guy is: a Nobel Prize–winning chemist. I'm not buying his notoriety here.

Unless he appeared on Dr. Oz—who came in sixteenth. Or on Oprah, who somehow came in forty-sixth!

Which just goes to show you how quickly you lose leverage once you're no longer on TV every day.

How would you like to win the Nobel Prize for your staggering work as a medical genius who has devoted your entire life to research that will save other human lives, but lose a trust competition to a fucking Canadian game show host?

U-S-A! U-S-A!

Take it from a famous actor: we shouldn't be on this list. Why?

Because we suck.

We're only good at memorizing lines and staring at ourselves in the mirror. The only things we can be trusted to do are lie about our age and how great our current project is. We care more about our frown lines than we do about melting ice caps. And we may have stopped wearing fur and promised not to eat meat anymore, but if there's a new neck cream that's made out of seal semen and actually gets rid of wrinkles? Hand us the baseball bats, 'cause we're heading for the beach.

The top ten spots on that list should consist of firefighters and soldiers. Police officers and nurses. Teachers and EMTs and community service volunteers. People who do dangerous and devoted work. People who live their lives thinking about helping others.

Actors don't think about anyone except other actors who are getting paid more than they are. Or have better plastic surgeons. And bigger houses.

Okay, I'm painting with a very big brush here. Not every actor is a cunf or a dink. And a lot of them have spent part of their fame raising a ton of money for many great charitable causes. Which as far as I'm concerned makes them very cool.

Listen, I thought getting famous would make ME cool. It didn't. It put me in rooms with cool people where I usually ended up making a fool of myself. Fate? Probably. Reminding me to never forget from whence I came: the attic of that two-and-a-half-decker at 1 Benefit Terrace in Main South, Worcester, Mass.

Believe me, I've never gotten over the thrill of being around show business legends. Every couple of years when I'm at a charity gala or awards show and hear someone say, "Hey, Denis—how's things?" and turn around to find Tony Bennett waiting for an answer, my knees buckle. Once a year at least I'm in the same room with Robert De Niro, and he always has a cell phone photo or two he wants to show me. He scrolls and I smile.

It never gets old. And I hope it never does.

But like I said: fame is a disease. It makes rich assholes born on third base think they hit a triple. It turns action movie airheads into budget-cutting icons. But one way or another, the flawed mighty always fall. By declaring bankruptcy on forty failing properties but not their own pussy-groping soul. Or marrying a Kennedy and then knocking up the maid.

As a celebrity doctor, diagnosing this fame flu is my area of expertise. So I'm going to call it My Shit Don't Stink Disease. MSDS for short. And I tell all my patients who suffer from MSDS the same thing: Yes it does. As a matter of fact, your shit stinks so bad they can smell it on fucking Mars. MSDS hits famous actors and athletes. Presidents and preachers. Even Diego from *Ice Age*.

Whenever I feel the symptoms of MSDS fever coming on, I always recall that old proverb: "Physician, heal thyself." Which I'm trying my best to do. What pill do I prescribe? Hanging out with people far more famous than I am. That seems to put me right back in my proper place.

Let me give you an example . . .

Nothing prepared me for being this awesome.

—BILL MURRAY

LADIES & GENTLEMEN, PLEASE WELCOME—ROD STEWART

I was asked to host an event billed as Fashion Rocks several times during the 2000s. The show was sponsored by Condé Nast and raised money for various causes each year through a live concert melding music stars and famed fashion designers, which was televised around the world.

The first one was held at the Royal Albert Hall in London, cohosted by Elizabeth Hurley and me to benefit The Prince's Trust, with seventeen performers and seventeen fashion designers all on one stage. The show was broadcast live on TV in Europe—meaning entrances and exits were timed right down to the very second, and the performers were ferried off and on stage at a breakneck pace, with pauses only for the occasional two- or three-minute commercial breaks. My old friend, acting partner, and future *Rescue Me* costar John Scurti was my personally chosen cowriter for that concert, feeding me lines and ideas as the evening unfolded.

And it went swimmingly.

Including a gag John handed me seconds before a live backstage interview with Michael Stipe, who had chosen to wear a mask of powder blue fluorescent eye makeup that covered his eyes and nose and wrapped around the sides and back of his shaven head. It was quite bright, and painstakingly applied.

Scurti saw the getup and, as the camera was about to roll, walked over and whispered a few words into my ear. Thus leading to my first on-camera question for Michael: "Hey man, what happened? Did you blow a Smurf?"

The line got a huuuge laugh, including one from Stipe himself. When I met Prince Charles after the show, he even referenced the gag and began guffawing all over again. That was an unexpected show business thrill—the Crown Prince of England discussing a blow job joke. Don't get much better than that.

The evening was a massive success, and the following year Condé Nast decided to make it an annual show and bring it to the United States using a live-to-tape approach. This time with me hosting solo.

In 2004 at Radio City Music Hall, my dressing room was located just off the stage, where Scurti sat at a computer coming up with new joke ideas based on the flow of the show, and where I had quick access to him and my cigarettes. It wasn't a large room, but it was big enough for us to commiserate momentarily after I had introduced an act.

Nerves were not a factor. I'd already played Radio City on my own, and one of the singular greatest thrills of my career happened there. The stage has three elevated platforms that can each descend thirty feet below stage level. As we were introduced, the band and I were already in place—unseen by the audience—and began playing the opening chords to "The Asshole Song" two stories below. Slowly but surely we rose up into view as the crowd went crazy. They exploded again as we went into the first chorus because—unplanned by us—our stage designer had twenty-five-foot-high letters light up behind us, spelling out the word ASSHOLE in bright, sparkling white. The entire band shared a huge smile and then finished what may have been the loudest, most exuberant version of the tune we ever gave.

Turns out we had another surprise on Rod Stewart night. The audience was not made aware in advance of the fact that Ron Wood would be appearing onstage to play guitar as Rod sang "Maggie May" and "Stay with Me." First I would introduce Rod and he would sing a number from his current album. Then there would be a three-minute commercial break, during which Rod would change outfits and I would go back onstage to introduce him and Ron.

I hadn't met Rod Stewart before. I missed him at sound check that afternoon and, so far during the course of my career, had never had the opportunity to make his acquaintance. But let me just ruminate for a few paragraphs on Rod—one of the greatest and most unique voices in the history of rock 'n' roll.

I first became enamored of his talent in 1971 when his solo album *Every Picture Tells a Story* came out, followed very quickly by the Faces' most recent album, featuring Rod on vocals. Two great works in one short year. Giving us within an eight-month span the now classic songs "Maggie May," "Reason to Believe," "(I Know) I'm Losing You," and—as if those three killers weren't enough—"Stay with Me."

I was also a rabid Boston Bruins hockey fan, and the TV broadcasts of their games used the intro of "(I Know) I'm Losing You" as the Bruins theme song. Someone in the Bruins organization was hip to the current hottest tunes.

At that time, my older brother Johnny and I lived in the basement of our parents' new ranch house in the Hadwen Park neighborhood of Worcester, Massachusetts. We shared a small room next to the water heater. I've written and spoken about that room numerous times; it was very cramped and covered in paneling. The walls, the ceiling, the closet—every single inch was paneled.

My parents loooooved paneling. If they could have paneled the backyard, they would have. The whole interior of the house was shrouded in it. The two upstairs bedrooms, the living room we weren't really allowed to sit in because the furniture was "too nice" and encased in plastic—even the one bathroom we all shared had tile in the shower, wallpaper on one wall, and the rest? You guessed it: paneling.

I never understood the theory behind covering your best furniture with plastic. That's like buying a Ralph Lauren suit, keeping it in a giant see-through ziplock bag, and bringing it out to show everyone during Thanksgiving, as if to say, "Isn't this nice? Doesn't it look expensive? Too expensive to actually wear, right? Here. Take a picture of me holding it and then it goes right back into the closet."

So my brother Johnny and I slept in what was essentially an eight-by-sixteen-foot wood-paneled coffin. The only part of our cellar bedroom that managed to escape such seventies-style, Irish American interior design was the floor, which sported a basic worn-out yellow batch of indoor/outdoor carpeting. It was tight quarters and had only a sliver of low light that managed to snake in for maybe two hours per day through a tiny, rectangular, ground-level window that sat close to the ceiling.

But we had our own entrance—the basement door. Which led to the backyard and an alley out to the street, so we could come and go as we pleased—which is important when you're fourteen years old and already smoking, drinking, and chasing girls. We also had our own refrigerator, an old late-fifties rat-box that had seen better days but served as my parents' storage space for "guest" beer—the good stuff they'd serve when we had visitors.

My brother and I drank that beer as if it was holy water. Which in a way it was. Because we'd already decided the Catholic school we were serving time in was preaching a bunch of impractical bullshit.

Fuck the church. That dirty downstairs room was our sanctuary. We could smoke and drink and parse the problems of the planet and puberty and pot and chicks and politics, while listening to Hendrix, the Who, the Stones, Marvin Gaye, Bowie, Zeppelin, Lennon, McCartney, Sly and the Family Stone, the Kinks—anyone and anything we wanted.

Sometimes Johnny and I would have conflicting appetites in music—for instance, he dug Crosby, Stills, Nash, & Not Nearly Enough Neil Young for my taste, but we both absolutely adored Rod Stewart and the Faces. In 1971, that meant playing both of their new albums incessantly. Until the grooves were so worn down, the needle was almost nipping the turntable.

By virtue of being broke and not well connected enough, we never had the chance to see Rod Stewart in his prime. As we got older, he became an elusive live concert get for us—our often empty wallets and his expensive show schedules never lining up.

Until 1993.

I had just gotten famous and was invited to be the only comedian to perform on MTV's critically acclaimed and extremely popular *Unplugged* series with my band the Assholes, from

No Cure for Cancer. "The Asshole Song" had become a hit, and several other comedy tunes on the album were getting airplay, plus a few new ones like "Life's Gonna Suck," "Love Barge," and "Save This," which would appear on my second album, *Lock 'N Load.*

The *Unplugged* episodes were filmed three at a time on a large Los Angeles soundstage. The set designers would slightly alter the look and lighting of the stage for each show, and the star dressing rooms were actually two large Winnebagos parked behind it. Our trio of shows consisted of Neil Young on Tuesday night, Rod on Wednesday, and my band on Thursday. So the Assholes and I decided to fly into L.A. early to rehearse and watch Rod tape his *Unplugged.*

Which was a tremendous mistake.

Rod took the crowd on a tour of his greatest hits, but what really stunned us was the magnitude of his charisma. With Ron Wood on guitar, Rod's signature sexy rasp brought the house down. It was a master class in professional musicianship, stage presence, and the tease: bringing the audience oh-so-slowly to the edge of teary-eyed orgasm on the slow numbers and then kicking their collective ass with a dose of rocket fuel on the big, rollicking hits.

Without ever. Missing. A note.

It was a powerful reminder that no matter where the musical times may lead us—and what style of Auto-Tuned, lip-sunk technocrap may temporarily take over the airwaves—the artists who really gain longevity all share the same DNA: live chops.

The only break Rod took in two hours of top-notch entertainment came at the end of each song when he and Ronnie would quickly gulp down some water out of red Solo cups and then kick off the next number. Watching Rod perform put a pit in our stomachs—because the next night we'd be up on that same stage trying to entertain thousands with my much weaker set of raspy talents on lead vocals.

Rod's Rock and Roll Hall of Fame voice has been described as "bedroom soul meeting street-smart balls." The only part of that phrase you could apply to my voice would be the word "balls," as in "I can't believe this guy has the balls to get up in front of people and sing."

So we scurried away before the encore without going backstage to meet Rod and Ronnie, all of us Assholes riding to the hotel feeling more than a little queasy.

The next day we arrived at the stage for sound check with almost no testosterone pissing through our nervous veins, wondering how we could ever have booked a gig following two such towering rock icons. We piled into the main Winnebago, and when our guitar player Adam Roth asked me for a bottle opener for his soda, the first four kitchen drawers I tried each had an empty vodka pint rattling around inside.

"What the fuck are all these empties from?" I asked the MTV producer who was giving us the run-of-show breakdown.

"Oh sorry, we forgot to clean them out," he answered. "Rod and Ronnie promised their wives they wouldn't drink last night, and we poured vodka into their onstage cups instead of water so they wouldn't get caught. Then the wives came backstage like right after the final number so we had to hide the evidence real fuckin' fast."

That fact brought us right back down to earth. We started

laughing our balls off so hard they dropped out of our scared stomachs and right back into their normal sack positions.

Turns out Rod and Ronnie were really just two regular guys trying to avoid getting busted by their better halves. Just like the rest of us. Needless to say, our nerves were immediately settled. Our *Unplugged* went great and got massive ratings, and the live version of "Life's Gonna Suck" became a cult classic.

Anyway, back to Radio City Music Hall in 2004. Where I still hadn't met Rod Stewart. Ron Wood and I had met and hung out together quite a bit at this point (which is part of another chapter, on the Rolling Stones). But on this night—on a show that included such music legends as Alicia Keys, Beyoncé, and Usher—Rod Stewart was the only one I didn't have the chance to meet face-to-face before the eight o'clock curtain. His dressing room was floors above my little nook off the side of the stage.

At one point I saw him in the distance down a hallway, greeting a clearly nervous Beyoncé, who took a few pictures with him. I was about to make my way toward them when the stage manager grabbed me and said it was time to kick things off.

As I said thirty-three paragraphs ago (sorry, my mind does wander), this show was live to tape, meaning it might as well be a live concert because the only time the director would call "CUT!" would be for a major fuckup. Otherwise, the few breaks in the two-hour extravaganza would be for commercials they would insert later on. My job as host was to keep the audience laughing after each artist finished and while the stage crew swept one set away and placed the next band's stuff in position.

The first four or five acts did great. Avril Lavigne, the Black Eyed Peas, the Goo Goo Dolls guy. Alicia Keys had the crowd in the palm of her hand. Usher had them dancing and swooning.

Beyoncé MURDERED the room. MURDERED it. Killed it and skinned it and buried what was left.

As I stepped up to the mike to introduce Rod Stewart for his first number, I briefly got a gander of him in the wings and wondered if he was worried about following her.

Nope. He had a smile on his face, chatting happily away with a P.A., and drinking some water (vodka?).

So I said his name: "Ladies and gentlemen, please welcome . . . ROD STEWART!"

And the place was resurrected. THAT is the sign of a real star. Beyoncé had destroyed the room a scant few moments before, but just the mention of Rod Stewart's name brought six thousand souls right back to life and onto their feet.

It was amazing to watch.

Which I only did for a few seconds because I had to go check in with Scurti, who was still sitting at the computer and watching Rod's performance on our backstage monitor. He was about to hand me an idea for a Beyoncé joke when we were interrupted by an attractive woman bearing a bunch of clothes on wooden hangers:

"I'm so sorry to waltz in, but would it be all right if Rod Stewart changes outfits in here during the commercial break? His dressing room's on the fifth floor and it would just be impossible for him to get all the way up there and back down in time for his second entrance."

John and I looked at each other and I said: "No problem." We acted like it was the most normal thing in the world. Matter of fact, we barely paid attention. As if having a rock legend take over our space was something that happened to us all the time. "Hey, whatever Rod needs," I said. Like I knew him already.

She thanked us and then hung a canary yellow sport coat, neon orange dress shirt, and a pair of jeans worth more than my father ever made in a year on the hooks next to my stuff. Then she tenderly placed a pair of blood orange sneakers with neon orange stripes on the floor below, said thank you oh so much, and left.

So Scurti and I did what any normal person would under the circumstances. We waited about half a second—just to make sure she was gone—and then ran over to the clothes and stared at them. Focused in like two fashion detectives in search of some kind of clothing clue, we felt the jacket and were in awe of how soft it was. We touched the shirt: even softer than the jacket. Then we caressed the jeans, which were like silk. Like, silky silk. Like, silken silky silk.

We were still smiling and stroking Rod's jeans like two sixteen-year-old girls when Scurti said, "Hey, before we grab our shit and give Rod the room, let me show you a couple of joke ideas for the finale." And so we crossed over to the table and sat down in front of his laptop when the crowd erupted in applause and we realized Rod must have finished his first number, so we looked at the monitor when BOOM!

The door flew open and in rushed Rod Fucking Stewart. With a glass of wine in his hand.

Downing a huge slug of it as he entered. Then saying this: "Hello, Denis! How's it goin', mate?"

Rod Stewart knew my name. Rod Stewart SAID my name. I wanted to whip out my cell phone and call my brother. Instead, I decided to answer Rod and move to leave when he whipped off his jacket and vest, took another slug of wine, and said this: "You lads don't mind me changin' in here, do ya?"

And as I muttered, "Not at all," he kicked off his shoes, pulled off his tie, and started unbuttoning his shirt as he said this: "Denis, are you bringin' me and Ronnie straight out or doin' some time before us?"

He said my name again! Holy shit. I really wanted to call my brother now.

Instead I said, "Whatever you, y'know—whatever you want, Rod. This is John, by the way."

"Hallo, Johnny Boy. Bring us right up then, Den. Ronnie's pre-set so when the curtain opens the crowd'll see him revealed and go fuckin' crazy."

He called me Den. Wow. Only my family and my wife call me that. My brother was getting a phone call before this night was over. He would FLIP OUT.

Listen, at this point in my career I'd met and even worked with a lot of monumental movie stars—De Niro, Dustin Hoffman, Clint Eastwood—and hung out with many of my musical heroes, like the Stones and Elvis Costello and Willie Nelson, not to mention become friends with my personal comedy kings George Carlin and Richard Pryor.

But each and every time I meet someone from such a talented stratosphere, I'm still very much impressed. I shoot right back to that basement bedroom where my brother and I were inspired by these people and spent hour after hour listening to or watching them, and then day after day discussing their work.

Meanwhile, Rod kept removing clothing.

He took off his shirt and in one fell swoop, for what felt like less than a nanosecond, unbuckled his belt, dropped his pants around his ankles, and stepped out of them.

Rod Stewart was now standing buck naked in front of us. Let me repeat that: Rod Stewart.

Naked.

Cock and Balls naked.

And then Ass—because he turned around.

And then Cock and Balls again as he decided to gulp down the remainder of his wine and WALK TOWARD US! Scurti and I froze in seated positions as Rod Stewart's Crotch waltzed across the room, headed right for our table.

This is as good a time as any to discuss The Unwritten Guys' Rule of Looking at Another Guy's Cock:

You just. Never. Do it.

In a hockey locker room with twenty-five guys undressing and twenty-four wangs for your eyes to accidentally glimpse— you avert your gaze. In a shared backstage dressing room, you quickly look elsewhere. ANYwhere. Your shoes, your shirt, your cell phone.

When I do arena concerts, my band comes with me and that's a minimum of eight guys plus me changing before and after a show. But even among such old friends you DO NOT STARE AT THE DICKS.

It's not always easy. With so much manhood flailing around in such crowded confines, your line of sight is bound to find an occasional cock in its crosshairs. And the polite thing to do is look away. Or make immediate eye contact with the owner. And start talking about sports or chicks or booze—anything except what just happened.

Nobody ever wrote this rule down. Nobody makes an announcement when you turn thirteen. Your father doesn't pass it along as important inside info while he's teaching you how to drive. It's just understood: you don't focus on the dicks.

A lesson I've learned so well that even when given the chance to notice another celebrity sausage, I abstain. I once took a piss shoulder-to-shoulder with Jon Hamm in a men's room at the White House Correspondents' Dinner and walked away knowing only this:

A. He's taller than you think
B. He's a big St. Louis Cardinals fan
C. Don Draper has dreamy green eyes

Did I know Jon was holding twelve inches of Hamm ham in his paws? Nope. Just like you, I read about it in the papers a couple of years later. But imagine if I was the one who slipped that pole profile to a roomful of D.C. media mavens? I would've been banned from every famous men's room faster than Caitlyn Fucking Jenner. I'd be a VIP penis pariah.

But Rod Stewart's knob was no TV star skin flute. His was beyond even a Matt Damon major movie meat stick. Rod's was a legendary dong. A knob that had been famous for five fucking decades by the time I saw it.

Which I couldn't avoid doing because I was in a seated position. So Rod Stewart's rod was eye level as it approached me.

Not. My. Fault.

I have a celebrity sausage. And over the years I've caught a couple guys gazing at it and then quickly making eye contact with me to start talking about the hockey game we just played or the gig we just finished. No big deal. But my penis is a D-level celebrity when compared with Rod Stewart's. His is attached to an actual rock icon. His is in the Rock and Roll Hall of Fame. His hog is historic.

I almost felt an obligation to observe it and report back to the masses: *Hey, you wanna know what Rod Stewart's penis looks like?* If you had the opportunity to see Mick Jagger's member or Obama's beef whistle or Derek Jeter's johnson—wouldn't you give it a glance?

Not an ogle. Not a gawk. Not a wide, eagle-eyed glare. Just a glimpse.

This was my quandary as Rod Stewart approached us.

I have no idea what Scurti was doing during the next manic four seconds, but my brain started making my mouth mumble aloud to Rod about how big a fan I was and what a head of hair you have and blah blah blubbedy blah while I swear to Christ,

Rod's pecker was almost daring me to dial in on it: *Look at me, Leary—look at me—look at me now, take a good long look, look, LOOK!*

But my mind was insistent on *eye contact eye contact eye contact* with Rod! And my mouth was still mumbling and Rod's schlong was still screaming *LOOKIT ME, LOOKIT ME, LOOK, LOOK, LOOK*, so—I looked at it.

I didn't give it a glance. Not even a glimpse. Wayyy shorter than even a half-glimpse. It was such a short view I'd have to invent a new word for it: a "glampse."

I glampsed it.

For maybe a zeptosecond—which is one sextillionth of a second—which is not enough time to really notice anything other than the fact that, yes, it's a penis. And when I swiftly returned my eyes up to Rod's, he seemed to know: this guy just glampsed my junk.

But instead of saying anything about that, he downed the rest of his wine, bopped the goblet onto the table, and said: "You can sell that on eBay, boys!" Then he turned around and headed back toward his clothing.

I did not get any descriptive details about Rod Stewart's cock. As it turns out, a zeptosecond is so small an amount of time, your mind can't measure what it sees other than to register the object in general: it was a dick. Not famous or massive or odd or small or anything except: a human penis.

That's all I could get.

But I will admit that once Rod was walking away, I took a good long fucking look at him and I can tell you this with 100% absolute certainty: the guy has a great ass.

I've never stared at another man's ass longer. It had to be seven seconds. That may sound like a long time, but hey—fuck you. I saw it and you didn't: his ass looked firm and round and tight—like two oversized grapefruits walking in rhythm.

I turned to see what Scurti was doing and guess what: same as me. Staring at Rod Stewart's famous, fine ass.

And the man was in great shape. He was fifty-nine at the time and had the body of a guy in his thirties. We watched him dress as he said, "Once we're done you'll come back on to outro us, yeah?"

"Oh yeah," I said. "I'll let the audience react for a bit, I'm sure you guys'll get a standing O."

"Well, we shall see, won't we?" he said with a charming smile.

Goddamn, I loved this man. Not just his ass—his whole being.

Then, in what seemed like a flash, Rod had his silky jeans, orange shirt, yellow jacket, and blood orange sneakers on and was saying this: "See ya out there, Den!"

And off he went. Leaving Scurti and me alone. I looked at him and raised my eyebrows, waiting for a response.

It's important to note here that John Scurti is a gifted member of that rare breed of actors who are so talented, almost every word of dialogue that trips from their tongues seems to be immediately transformed into spun gold. As Lou on *Rescue Me* he captured people's hearts, and I count him as the kind of performer no successful TV series can work without. He can make you laugh, cry, and fear for your life—all in one scene. Brilliant and beguiling. Comedy, drama—small scenes and lengthy monologues—it matters not what assignment he has to tackle. Scurti can make it sound like the dialogue was delivered to him directly from the gods above. And he goes deep—deep enough to improvise in character and make the words he was given disappear, to be replaced by ones funnier, prettier, heavier, and just plain better.

He's also a terrific writer and one of the most hilarious people on the planet. Having known him for decades, there was never a time—on set or off, funeral or celebration, casual dinner or formal gala event—where he wasn't able to utter something that would make me laugh my ass off.

Except right now. He just stared back at me: speechless.

The stage manager stuck his head in the door and said, "We gotta go, Denis—we haven't had a time stoppage all night, let's not start now." And so off I went. It was true—the show so far had been a dream: smooth as Rod's jeans and without a single mistake. Not once had the director been forced to yell "CUT!"

Rod took his place at center stage behind the curtain as I strolled confidently to my mark. The lights came on and the audience applauded—their excitement was palpable and infectious. Six thousand true music fans. Twelve thousand eager eyes. I took a dramatic beat and—like the true professional I am—said: "Ladies and gentlemen, once again—Cock Stewart!" To absolute and utter silence. Until this: "CUT!"

I felt like my head was going to explode. *Cock? I said Cock Stewart?* A ripple of nervous laughter coursed through the first few rows of the crowd. I froze in place and then just announced: "Rod. Rod Stewart."

But to no avail: the mike had gone dead—apparently, somewhere during the words "once again." So nobody heard me say Cock Stewart—except the first few rows of the crowd. But Rod was only a few feet behind me, hidden behind the curtain yet close enough to have heard what I said.

I wanted to pull back the curtain and explain to him what happened—that it was just a nervous accident and not a joke —but a TV technician wearing a headset was suddenly in front of me, replacing my mike with a shake of his head and a smile as he held up five fingers and said, "Bad mike." Apparently he hadn't heard my mistake either. I exhaled deeply. Calmed down. Waited for him to finish. Which he did by whispering, "Don't say 'cock' this time" as he held up four fingers and counted "four, three, two, one," and pointed at me: action.

This time I took a big juicy pause and double-checked my brain to make sure the proper words came out of my mouth and this is what I said: "Ladies and gentlemen, please welcome back, Co-Rod Stewart."

And the opening notes of "Maggie May" began. *Jesus Christ, I almost said Cock again.* And the crowd went crazy. *What the fuck is wrong with me?* And then the curtain opened, the lights blasted up, and they saw Ronnie Wood. And they went even crazier.

Ronnie and Rod killed. Just completely demolished the place. And I went onstage afterward and said, "Rod Stewart, everybody!" Not Cock. Not Co-Rod. Rod. And then I said, "How about Ron Wood, ladies and gentlemen?" They both gave me a quick glance. It was hard to tell if Rod was pissed at me with six thousand people giving him a standing ovation. I figured a backstage apology would be the best move. But unfortunately that didn't happen.

Because I never saw Rod Stewart in person again. Which has become a theme in many of my interactions with famous rock stars.

In this case, Rod didn't show up at the after-party, where Scurti and I laughed about our experience and discussed just how much a wine goblet from a rock god might be worth online. In the end, Scurti kept the glass. And I kept my memory of Cock Stewart. Which—when you think about it—is actually a really great name for a rock 'n' roll singer.

When I called my brother, he totally agreed.

Since that night, every time I see Rod being welcomed to the stage for a TV appearance or listen as a song of his is played on the radio, I think of him as Cock Stewart.

And now, so will you. You're welcome.

Even with this kind of damage already done in celebrity circles, some of my fans only half-jokingly still want me to run for the Oval Office. Do you really want a president who might accidentally mention cock on TV? Oh wait—we already have that guy. Who referred to his own.

On purpose.

Listen, we have many examples of famous people who hung their Hollywood hats on some political star and not only pulled it off, but did so with graceful aplomb. On both sides of the aisle.

Al Franken and Fred Thompson. Jesse Ventura and Ronald Reagan. Oscar winner Glenda Jackson served in Parliament for twenty-three years, earning plaudits for tirelessly representing her constituents and staying devoted to their cause.

Child star Shirley Temple became a trusted American foreign ambassador and served as a highly respected delegate to the United Nations General Assembly for Republican and Democratic administrations alike, drawing much acclaim as a bipartisan patriot.

Will Trump one day join that pantheon? The jury is out. But I sure won't. Why?

Keep reading.

You're not famous until my mother knows who you are.

—JAY LENO

BEYONCÉ AND ME

Yes. You got that chapter title right. It's not a typo. I know Beyoncé.

And if I ever need a lesson in fame humility, hanging around with her hands it to me tenfold. She's not just famous. Queen Bey's an artist so beloved that she occupies exalted air. And very deservedly so.

Let me tell you how we first met.

The 2008 Fashion Rocks concert at Radio City was probably the biggest one I ever did. The money raised was earmarked for Stand Up to Cancer and the lineup was absolutely insane: Carrie Underwood, Mary J. Blige, Rihanna, Debbie Harry, Fergie, the Black Eyed Peas, Justin Timberlake, Miley Cyrus, Natasha Bedingfield, Ciara, Duffy, Leona Lewis, Mariah Carey, Ashanti, Keyshia Cole, Kid Rock, Solange, Keith Urban, Pussycat Dolls, and Lynyrd Fucking Skynyrd.

Plus, reprise video performances from previous Fashion Rocks events, including Bryan Adams tearing up the Royal Albert Hall in 2003, David Bowie returning to the stage after a long absence to sing "Life on Mars" alone and "Five Years" in tandem with

Arcade Fire from 2005, and Elton John hosting the show in 2006.

And three different helpings of Beyoncé: Beyoncé doing a tribute to Etta James. Beyoncé doing a duet with Justin Timberlake on the old Marvin Gaye and Tammi Terrell tune "Ain't Nothing Like the Real Thing." And Beyoncé joining some of the other female stars for a version of the charity single "Just Stand Up."

My daughter, Devin, was sixteen at the time and was not only the world's biggest Beyoncé fan, but had never seen her live. So as the host of the show, I made sure she and five of her Beyoncé fanatic friends had front row seats.

Which got me major Dad points. Not to mention the ultra-major Dad points I would earn if I could introduce Devin to her musical hero, which I figured was bound to happen since Queen Bey was doing so much material in the course of the show, plus the red carpet, which Devin and I would also be walking.

Somewhere in that five-hour window I was bound to meet Bae and bring Devin to her attention. Even though Beyoncé had performed at the earlier Cock Stewart Fashion Rocks, we never met face-to-face or stood anywhere near each other. Her intros that night were done by an offstage announcer, and she ghosted as soon as her final number was finished. But on this particular night I was not leaving the building without making sure she knew who I was.

And if all else failed, there was a secret backdoor escape route all the celebrities would be taking as we left the event and went to the massive after-party. Dev and I could always just wait there until Beyoncé headed out and casually introduce ourselves—or even better yet, have Beyoncé stop and compliment my performance.

Which I figured was going to happen, because I had a fantastic gag set up as the centerpiece of my hosting job.

My talented friend and highly respected comedian Jeff Cesario was cowriter on this gig, and among the bevy of great ideas he had was one playing off the fashion angle. My stylist, Sam Spector, mentioned to us that several designers were willing to comp me clothes if I wore their stuff on-camera during the concert.

Jeff's pitch was: I would walk out and explain to the audience that each time I mention a designer's name, I'd get to keep the clothes I was currently wearing.

All of it. Head to toe.

At the end of the opening monologue, I did that setup and finished with, "For instance, this suit is from John Varvatos and now—it's all mine."

A few performances later I came out in a different suit, said, "Thank you, Hugo Boss!" as I modeled it and pointed comically down at my shoes while purring, "Created by Kenneth Cole, ladies and gentlemen." Then I introduced the Bryan Adams kickass performance from the first Fashion Rocks.

The payoff came a little later when I stumbled out in two-thousand-dollar, six-inch-high Christian Louboutin stiletto heels—wearing a front-plunging, nine-thousand-dollar Gucci gold gown, Harry Winston diamond earrings worth seventy-five grand each, and a chunky Cartier diamond bracelet that cost twice as much as my daughter's college education.

After walking with some difficulty to center stage, I stood at the mike for a moment and tried to fix my double nip-slip. Which was almost impossible.

Then—frozen there in all my designer glory—I sighed with exasperation and said, "My wife called."

Big laugh. BIG laugh.

But the story of that outfit starts earlier in the evening.

I had asked Sam to find me something I could get in and out of quickly—since I'd have exactly twelve minutes to travel from the stage to my fifth-floor dressing room, change, and head back down again. It would be the 2003 Bryan Adams video, which was about four minutes of rock-and-roll fury from his airtight three-piece band, then a Beyoncé live performance introduced by my prerecorded voice, then a commercial break before my voice intro'd Mary J. Blige.

And after the dress gag, I'd have about the same amount of time to get back upstairs and put on another suit.

Sam came up with a dress that looked so small when he first pulled it out of his bag that I thought it was a tube top. "It's Keira Knightley's gown from *The Pirates of the Caribbean* premiere," he explained. "It's kind of iconic because she got a lot of press in that dress."

Keira Knightley? Holy shit. I'd seen the pictures of her in it—who hadn't? They were everywhere after that event. She looked stunning. And small. As did the dress Sam handed me.

It was very gold. And very shiny. And tiny as hell.

"I can't fit into that fucking thing, Sam—plus, it's way too fancy. I need a funny dress."

Cesario was in the room and very much in agreement with me:

"All he needs is a gag dress—something that's not so" —and here he searched for the correct comedy expert word—"um, clingy."

"Yes, not too clingy," I chimed in. "Clingy isn't funny on a guy."

Leave it to Sam Spector to put us in our place.

"Listen, guys, clingy IS funny. I know fashion and I know what's funny about fashion. If you walk out there in any old dress, this crowd won't laugh. If you walk out there in a glamorous, close-fitting gown—all dolled up like the other girls onstage tonight—you will get a LOT of laughs. Because it looks like a dress every woman would kill to wear. This dress is funny. The fact that Keira made the dress famous already—and that a man is wearing it—makes it all the more hilarious. Same thing with the accessories—shoes, earrings, the clutch—they all make it funnier because they're things women really want to wear. Now go try on the gown."

Five words no one on earth had ever said to me before: *go try on the gown.*

Which I did. My dressing room was small and overpopulated so the easiest place to change was the men's room across the hall. There was a security guard outside that door to guarantee me privacy. I changed into the gown and took a glance at myself in the mirror: I looked like Bruce Jenner before he became Caitlyn. Only with a much bigger nose.

But guess what: as soon as I walked back into my dressing room—Jeff, Sam, the hair and makeup girls, and the security guard outside my door—all started laughing their asses off. Sam was right. And full of other info after I peeled off the gown and stood there in my boxers.

"But you can't wear boxers underneath. It ruins the line of the dress. You need to wear a thong."

A thong?

"If you wear a thong your balls won't be cold. If you go commando, expect a draft. And the dress is so clingy, people will see the outline of your penis through it."

I sighed with acceptance.

"It's a very soft satin thong, so your balls will be cozy."

Your balls will be cozy.

Five more words I'd never heard before. Having just learned he was an expert about drag, I took Sam's advice. By the way, that's really what a thong is when it's worn by a man: a ball cozy.

So, come the appointed time during the show, I'd have to rush offstage, take an elevator to the fifth floor, grab the dress, jewels, and thong, run into the men's room, and change from Denis into Denise. I stood there in my boxers mulling over these facts and the insane timing of it all.

That's when I heard this:

"Omigod, I wish I had your legs," my makeup artist, Amy, said.

"What?" I replied.

"They're so long and lean. You'd look great in a miniskirt."

Wait a minute—what?

"Maybe you should shave them."

"You're shittin' me, right?"

"No. They are unbelievable. I'd kill to have them. But they won't look their best unless you shave them."

"I'm not shaving my fucking legs, Amy!"

Cesario chimed in: "You do have amazing legs, man. Seriously."

Sam: "I'm gonna get you a miniskirt for later in the show."

Amy: "You should definitely shave if you wear a skirt."

Cesario: "Totally. Otherwise it'll ruin the look."

"GUYS! FORGET IT! I'M NOT WEARING A MINISKIRT! EVER! AND STOP STARING AT MY LEGS!"

Cesario: "Dude—you have girl legs. Embrace it. You know how hilarious you would look in a miniskirt? Or a bikini?"

I could see the comedy future flashing before my eyes. So I drew a line in the sand:

"I am never—repeat: never ever EVER—getting a bikini wax."

It was easy to notice that Jeff, Sam, and Amy knew otherwise. In a battle between bikini wax and belly laughs, belly laughs would always win. Imagine me onstage at Radio City Music Hall one day in a bikini and high heels with perfectly oiled and long, spray-tanned, girl-type legs. Just for a sec.

Got the image?

Good.

Glad I could be of comedy service.

Now back to our present situation: cut to halfway through the 2008 show when it's time for me to make my move.

I introduced the Bryan Adams video from the first Fashion Rocks back in 2003. He stole the show that night. Just him, his bass player, and his drummer—three great musicians who sounded like ten. Bryan sang "The Only Thing That Looks Good on Me Is You" as a series of statuesque, drop-dead-gorgeous models strutted by in designer duds.

Bryan ran around that stage like a madman, his band gunning the beat behind him as he brought the audience to its feet—a performance for the ages, and one so electric it still shot adrenaline through Radio City five years later.

While it was playing I rushed into the elevator and up to the fifth floor.

Cut to the men's room: I'm inside a stall tearing off my Hugo Boss suit and stepping into the Gucci gown, crowning it all off by pulling on my testicle cozy.

I had the earrings and bracelet on already. And about five minutes left before I had to be back downstairs. Sam was stationed outside the men's room door keeping watch and listening in case I needed help or advice.

Turns out, I badly needed both.

I don't know how the hell anyone can wear a thong and feel comfortable.

Especially if you have balls.

Mine just wouldn't fit. I wriggled and wrangled and adjusted and readjusted and re-readjusted and no fucking go—whenever I got my gonads tucked inside the insanely tiny pouch, my penis refused to be a part of the plan. And vice versa.

"Hurry up, Denis—they're asking for you downstairs!" Sam said from the hallway.

ARRRGGH!

The clock was ticking and my cock wasn't cooperating and I grunted in frustration as I heard Sam enter the bathroom, so I screamed: "GODDAMMIT! MY BALLS WON'T STAY IN UN-LESS MY COCK STAYS OUT—AND MY COCK ONLY STAYS IN IF MY BALLS SPILL OUT THE SIDE!"

I threw open the door of the stall and came flying out to confront him with: "NOT TO MENTION MY ASS FEELS LIKE IT'S BEING FLOSSED WITH A FUCKING EXTENSION CORD!"

To which Justin Timberlake said, "Um—okay." I repeat: Justin Timberlake.

THE Justin Timberlake.

Who was, apparently, just trying to take a piss.

And who now had an upset, on-the-verge-of-tears, bejeweled, grown fucking man in a gown and high heels staring at him.

I'd never met Justin before. And I've never seen him since.

Probably because the next thing I said was this: "HEY, JUSTIN! Huuuuge fan. Listen—you've probly dressed up like a chick before, right? Did you go commando or thong? Here, let me take the thong off and you tell me if you can see the outline of my cock and ball sack through the dress."

So I pulled up the gown and started pulling down the thong.

"Can I ask you another question—and please, be brutally honest—do I have girl legs?"

Then I modeled for him. Thong in hand. Gown pulled up. Twirled around slowly. Smiled. And said: "Well?"

Only one word can describe the look on Justin Timberlake's face: "troubled." With a capital *T.* And all he said was: "I, uh—I'd really like to help you out but, I don't—I've never—um—I gotta go."

And that was it. He left. Very quickly. And in came a security guard. *What the fuck?*

"Where's Sam?" I whined.

"Takin' a picture with Mary J. Blige," the guard explained. "Listen, man—you can't block off the men's room and you can't go upsetting big stars like Justin Fucking Timberlake. You do know that was him, right?"

"Of course I know he's Justin Fucking Timberlake! And now Justin Fucking Timberlake is gonna think I'm totally batshit crazy," I said. Standing there in my fabulous dress and glittering jewelry, holding my oh-so-satiny thong.

The guard gave me a glare. I gave him one back.

222 DR. DENIS LEARY

And then we both started laughing hysterically.

Needless to say, on went the ball cozy. And down the hall into the elevator went Denise.

Now for a couple of floors it was just me, Jeff, Sam, Amy, and a production assistant from the show. I was busy trying to get comfortable in my crotch and butt area, while also trying not to fall off my heels. Suddenly I had a whole new appreciation for what it's like to be a woman.

Walking in stilettos made me feel as though I was balancing on a steel circus high-wire, one that also ran right up my ass crack. My chest was exposed to the air-conditioning, which meant my nipples were harder than Vin Diesel's head as they popped against the top of my gown, and the diamond clusters on my ears started itching as they dragged each lobe closer to a collarbone.

Plus, everyone was staring at different parts of me. My tits, my legs, my dick, my ass—I was being objectified!

"Hey, guys," I said. "My eyes are up here."

"We're not worried about your eyes," Jeff explained.

The elevator doors opened up to reveal Kid Rock and Lynyrd Fucking Skynyrd. Beers in hand, headed up to their dressing rooms. Eight sets of eyes wider than super-sized Frisbees.

"Holy shit!" Kid Rock exclaimed. "You look hot, man."

One of the guys from Skynyrd looked me up and down: "Damn— lookit them little titties!" And then as we walked away I heard,

"Nice ass, sister!" and they chuckled their way onto the elevator as we rushed toward the wings.

It was truly a mind-bending moment.

Believe me, when I was in high school and dreaming of being famous one day, having my ass ogled by Lynyrd Fucking Skynyrd wasn't on my celebrity bucket list.

I felt slightly demeaned and disgusted.

I wanted to turn on my very high heels and scream, *Hey, Skynyrd! First of all, my tits ain't that small! For a tall skinny guy, I'm in pretty good shape and my tits are well defined! Second of all, you just said I had a nice ass but I guess that isn't good enough for you? Huh? Well, get a load of these legs, motherfucker! A lot of girls would KILL for these legs!*

Yeah. I was having some pretty strange thoughts.

My Irish was up and my temper was flaring. So it was becoming kind of clear: if I had been born a girl, I'd have great legs, a nice ass, and very small tits. So what? Keira had small tits and a fantastic ass and shorter legs than mine but was considered one of the hottest women on earth. Who needs big tits?

Not Keira. And not me!

Besides, I could always buy big tits. You can't really buy a nice ass unless you want a BIGGER ass. And long legs? God-given. Ain't no surgery for elongated gams. You either got 'em or you don't. And I do. So there. Fuck you, Lynyrd Skynyrd!

Yeah—I wasn't just having strange thoughts, I was suffering

through an actual full-blown identity crisis. But what happened next might have been even stranger.

I got to my appointed spot in the wings, ready to make a big entrance. The stagehands were still setting a Chevy Camaro SS V8 in place, from which Debbie Harry would appear during Fergie's performance of the Blondie hit "Call Me."

I glanced to my right and there was Debbie getting ready to climb inside. She saw me and stopped for a second, tilted her head, smiled, and blew me a kiss.

As she sat in the car and the door closed I was in a sudden teenage fog: at age nineteen, meeting Debbie Harry would have been an impossible idea for my friends and me, both male and female. Every guy I knew in the late seventies had a crush on her, and so did most of the girls.

My buddy Adam Roth was already a full-time rock-and-roll guitar player in a notorious Boston band called the Marshalls, and was lucky enough to have seen Debbie up close at CBGB's one night in 1976. And unable to stop talking about it for two years.

We were so enamored and obsessed with her that when our friend Michelle announced that the record store she worked in was about to get two life-sized cardboard cutouts of Debbie— one for the floor and one as a backup in case the first one got damaged—we begged and pleaded for her to let us have a Debbie.

Thankfully she gave in. But we had to come steal it after dark, at the rear door in an alley. It was like a bank heist.

Cut to me and Adam skulking through the backstreets of downtown Boston, making our way to his apartment with a one-dimensional Debbie Harry, who stayed upright in the living room for as long as Adam lived there. In 1978, I'd sometimes look at one-dimensional Debbie and wonder what it would be like if I ever had the chance to meet three-dimensional Debbie face-to-face. Would we have chemistry? Would there be heat between us? What would I say? What would I do?

Well, cut to me at Radio City circa 2008—now I knew: I'd be dressed as a woman and just standing there like a dumbfounded fool with two erect nipples and ten sore toes, shrugging. The only heat between us was the smell of another show business dream of mine going up in comedy smoke.

Then I heard a man's voice say, "Hey dude, I dig those shoes."

Turning around, I saw will.i.am just inches away, staring at my stilettos and admiring my glimmery bracelet. He took my wrist in one hand and ran his fingertips along the multiple diamond edges.

"Nice ice. You look fantastic. And that dress is just killer, baby."

I suddenly felt flush and very feminine. I smiled and gushed, "Thank you, will, that's so sweet of you to say that."

"I mean it, man. Love the earrings too. They make your eyes really pop."

I batted my fake eyelashes a little at that remark. And giggled a bit.

And suddenly turned into the world's biggest Black Eyed Peas fan.

And then I wondered why he hadn't mentioned my ass yet.

Maybe he hasn't seen it, I thought. *Turn around!* my brain whispered loudly to my body, *give him the full effect.*

I was in mid-twirl when another part of my brain piped in: *What the hell is wrong with you, Denis—you dim Irish donkey.*

I had a little interior mini-monologue with myself: *Hey, asshole— you ain't some hot young chick dressed to the nines and competing with a building full of A-list famous females; you're a man dressed as a woman for a comedy gag you gotta go out and do right now. WAKE THE FUCK UP!*

The outfit and my man-vanity were turning me into a seriously insane, attention-seeking mess. Just then I was yanked out of my reverie and returned to planet earth when I got my cue and had to head onstage, where—once they saw what I was wearing—the audience began to laugh. Like any truly addicted live performer will tell you, the sound of six thousand people about to bust a gut had me in comedy heaven—tits or no tits.

Smash-cut to an hour later: the show is over and I'm upstairs wearing my own clothes and hanging out with my daughter and her friends, who were very impressed by the evening's entertainment—especially the sight of me in my girlish getup. And Beyoncé. I'd almost forgotten about Beyoncé.

In all the excitement and quick-change running around, I realized I'd not only still never met the woman, but—more important—neither had Devin.

So once again we went rushing onto the elevator and down to the first floor, through a maze of hallways and tunnels until we came up into the secret exit area where all celebs and their entourages would be taking leave for the after-party.

But instead of leaving we stood off to the side, awaiting Queen Bey. One by one, celebs came coursing by, each saying "Hey, Denis!" or "You going to the party?" or some iteration of "You were great/hilarious/funny as shit tonight."

The girls were nervously chattering while I wondered if Beyoncé would mention my outfit, still stuck in man-vanity land over my girl legs and accoutrements.

I planned on not being first to bother her, since she was one of those icons constantly having people interrupt her or besiege her—and we were both celebrities after all, so I'd just play it cool, as if Devin and I were just waiting for someone else.

That was Plan A.

But if she did stop to talk, I'd go right into Plan B.

Which involved me laughing off her positive comments in a modest manner and then telling her how fantastic SHE was, and then if she insisted on talking some more about my performance, I'd say how great the audience was and mention my writer Jeff Cesario and my whole entourage, and then introduce Devin.

That seemed like a good plan when Devin walloped me in the arm and hushed into my face: "DAD!" And I turned to see Beyoncé with about five people behind her as she came down the hallway and idiotically blurted out way too loudly, "Beyoncé! You were awesome tonight!"

She looked up at me and smiled. A beaming smile.

A smile that clearly said, *Oh my God, it's YOU!*

I've seen that smile after my shows before, from famous people and not so famous people. It's a smile of recognition and appreciation. It's a smile reflecting the joy that person just experienced during my performance—a smile that reprises the happiness I've bestowed upon them with my multifaceted talent, cutting-edge wit, and professional dedication.

I was almost beside myself as Beyoncé, as if to validate my intuition, blurted out this:

"So were you, Bryan!"

She was still walking, so I said: "Thank you, Beyoncé!"

"I love your voice!" she said over her shoulder, as she and her entourage continued to walk past us.

Out the door.

Into her limo.

And drove away.

There was an awkward beat as I stood there—still waving.

There was another awkward beat as I turned back to Devin and HER entourage. The friends didn't know what to say.

But Dev did: "Dad, Beyoncé thought you were Bryan Adams."

This was a very important father/daughter situation. How I reacted would not only impact Devin right now, but possibly for years to come—maybe even permanently. And it could also have an effect on how Devin's friends saw her.

It was a very delicate moment. What some might call a teachable moment. And so, as a devoted father, I decided to do just that. Teach. I thought for a second, looked into my daughter's disappointed eyes, and carefully explained: "Hey—it's Beyoncé. If she thinks I'm Bryan Adams, then I'm Bryan Fucking Adams. Did you see his performance? He blew the roof off the place! Now c'mon, let's get our asses over to that after-party and see if Bryan can get Beyoncé to take a picture with you guys."

I was teaching them humility.

And how much of an amoeba fame can actually be. (I should have used the word "amoeba"; then I could have taught them a little science, too.)

If Beyoncé ran for president in our next election cycle, Devin and her friends would jump for joy and cast their ballots in advance. As would I. Imagine seeing our State of the Union delivered with a kickass chorus and fourteen backup dancers. Forget the dignity and decorum of the office. Trump certainly has. So did Bill Clinton. Meanwhile, if President Beyoncé sang the Bill of Rights in the Rose Garden one afternoon, every kid in this country would have it memorized by dinnertime.

Beyoncé 2020: Let the Drumbeat Begin.

But Leary 2020? That comedy dream would die under the weight of its own bloated expectations. Because this wasn't the first time I'd been mistaken for someone more talented than me. Not by a long shot.

And it sure wouldn't be the last.

You'd think that a famous rock star being married to a gorgeous supermodel would be one of the greatest things in the world.
It is.

—DAVID BOWIE

FAME (WHAT'S YOUR NAME? WHAT'S YOUR NAME?)

Just like my dad, I can look at my life and consider myself one of the luckiest men in America.

If you had told me in 1967 that a second son of Irish immigrants would end up standing next to the President of the United States at a Rose Garden celebration of the World Champion 2013 Red Sox?

I would assume you were dosed on LSD.

My mom always reminds me how proud she is of my success, while simultaneously making sure I keep my feet firmly on the ground. So my fame has never been allowed to go to my head.

One example: I'm sitting in my dentist's waiting area in New York City, plucking at my phone, avoiding eye contact with everyone else. And I hear someone say, "Hey, man."

So I look up to find Paul McCartney smiling down at me and saying sweetly, "I didn't wanna bother ya, but I just had to say hello."

Okay—freeze frame.

Let's ESPN this moment in my life: Paul McCartney. SIR Paul McCartney.

Who I first saw on TV in 1964. In the Beatles.

Even my parents were fans.

Is shaking my hand and smiling, having just apologized for bothering ME!

I slowly stand up so we're face-to-face, still shaking hands. Millions of musical questions are zipping into my head, six decades of great songs, thousands of meaningful moments in my life that his music underscored.

I had so many things I could say.

But I'm sure it comes as no surprise that what I chose to say was this: "Hey, Paul McCartney—what're YOU doin' here?"

"Um—gettin' my teeth cleaned."

He paused for a second, awaiting my next sentence—which turned out to be this: "Wow! Me too!"

Then there was another pause—and I could see the friendly light in Paul's eyes beginning to dim as he realized he was stuck in a hero worship situation, instead of a funny conversation with a fellow celebrity. So I said this: "Let me see how yours look!" While madly beaming at him.

"Um, okay," Paul replied.

He reluctantly offered a semi-wide smile—his Beatle teeth partially bared—and I went: "They look awesome! Soooo white! Did you get them whitened or are they always that white?"

The normal neurons in my brain asked the moron motors currently operating it: *Did he just say the word "white" three fucking times? Yes,* the moron motors responded, *and we may even say it a few more.*

Paul appeared to be a little taken aback. Then he said, "Let me see yours." So I bared my non-Beatle teeth.

Too widely, I'm sure.

Because Paul seemed to step back an inch or two as he said, "Very nice. Well, see you later, mate. Good luck."

And he left in what can only be described as: a bit of a rush.

For the first time I noticed the other patients in the room, and each expression seemed to say, *What the fuck was that?* One guy actually offered a slight eye-roll, shook his head at me, and smiled snarkily as he turned his attention back to a magazine.

The vibe in the room was clear: I'd blown it.

Totally blown the opportunity to become friends with a Beatle. One of only two Beatles left alive!

Upon immediate mental review, I realized how weird and clumsy our conversation had been. All down to my inability to avoid what I call Fan Panic.

As a doctor, I'm allowed to scientifically identify certain medi-

cal conditions, and Fan Panic is one I was actually first to diag-
nose and name: it's a series of anxiety-related reactions within
the brain and body that afflict patients upon meeting someone
they worship.

I've actually witnessed it myself: fans who stammer and/or
shake as they try to get an autograph or pose for a picture with
you.

So imagine how often Paul McCartney has found himself
dealing with Fan Panic. Every day. For the last fifty-something
years.

And then imagine his disappointment when he meets another
famous guy and thinks he's about to have a fairly decent, funny
little chat—and instead gets another boring dose of Panicky Fan
Face (one more diagnosis of mine).

Panicky Fan Face is when you look like a deer in the headlights
as someone famous finally stands in front of you. And I realized now that I had looked like the craziest deer in the brightest
high-beam headlights ever made.

So I did what you would have done after meeting a Beatle and
blowing it: I called my mom, skipping over the mistakes I'd just
managed to make and instead telling her how Paul McCartney—
THE Paul McCartney—had just walked up to say hello to me.

Her first response was significantly valid: "Did he think you
were someone else?"

That's the story of my famous life.

Since the very first time I walked down the street circa 1992 and started to notice some side-eye glances and long, excited stares from random passersby, the drug that is being famous was always dotted with built-in reality-check speed bumps for me.

Early on, I couldn't avoid learning lessons about just where I stood on the Hollywood ladder. I was walking through an airport in 1993 when a Panicky Fan Face appeared in front of me, hands trembling as he asked me for an autograph. Which I gladly signed.

Which almost immediately led to him pointing at my signature and asking, "What the hell does that say?"

"All the best comma Denis Leary," I explained.

The Panicky Fan Face quickly morphed into Angry Disappointment Visage as he snapped, "Goddammit! I thought you were Willem Dafoe. Someone said he was here."

And off he went, dropping the signed piece of paper into a trash can.

At first I was pissed. Willem Fucking Dafoe?

He's not funny. Or tall. Or even 100% Irish.

Plus, I was Denis Fucking Leary, motherfucker! Famous comedian. My name and face were all over the place. MTV. The movies. Books, magazines, TV, CDs. I was a multimedia monster about to become a showbiz legend.

Then I thought, *Hey, wait a minute. I might ALREADY be a legend. I'm being mistaken for an incredibly talented, Oscar-nominated actor. Respected for his striking dramatic work on the silver screen and the theatrical stage.*

And so was born a career's worth of me being Willem. And I can only hope vice versa.

While I'm at JFK airport hearing "Hey, you were fantastic in *Platoon*" or "I loooved *The English Patient*" and "You blew me away in *The Last Temptation of Christ*," I can only hope Willem's at LAX wincing as someone mentions how much they love "The Asshole Song." Or *Operation Dumbo Drop*.

And this happens everywhere on earth.

I was vacationing in Rome with my family once and stepped outside the hotel to have a smoke. Several people smiled and said *"Ciao!"* or *"Come va!"* or *"Buongiorno!"* as they walked past me in what seemed like a very enthusiastic manner. Clearly they were fans of mine, my fame having reached across the ocean. The smiles indicating how stand-up comedy and the cinema form a truly international language. That evening at dinner? The same thing. Except with smiles and *"Buonasera!"*

And the next day, the same love all over again. Until I went out to buy some cigarettes and the guy behind the counter said, "When you start smoking, Willem?"

Come to find out: I was staying in the same neighborhood where Dafoe and his new Italian bride, Giada Colagrande, lived.

There was no escaping the man.

Willem and I became even further intertwined after we both became members of the Spiderman family.

For years my Dafoe-by-default existence included airport security guards happily greeting me with "Hey, it's the Green Goblin!" almost every time I traveled. More than once I got eased through long TSA lines because an agent would tag me with a variation on the phrase "I loved you in *Spiderman*," as he or she would usher me away from the shoeless masses.

And I played right along, answering questions about what Tobey Maguire and James Franco were REALLY like, and—eventually—what a shame it was that there wouldn't be a *Spiderman 4*.

Then, in 2012, I got asked to play Captain Stacy—Emma Stone's fictional dad—in *The Amazing Spiderman*, a reboot of the franchise. And all hell broke loose in airports around the planet. Guards would begin to argue as I entered their area. Here's one actual exchange I heard between four TSA members at Chicago's O'Hare Airport in 2014:

"Hey, it's Captain Stacy!"

"Captain who? It's Green Goblin, asshole."

"Green Goblin's from the old *Spiderman*. Captain Stacy's from the new one. He's the chief of police."

"So the bad guy's now a GOOD guy? That's a kickass plot twist."

"It's not a plot twist, motherfucker. He's Emma Stone's dad."

"You're Emma Stone's dad?"

"His ID says his name is Leary."

"So who's got the fake name, you or Emma?"

There WAS a plot twist in the Denis & Dafoe Diaries a few years back when Willem did that Snickers commercial wearing a dress. Now every so often when I go through security I also have to hear about how bad I look when I'm hungry and how short and skinny my legs are. I tried explaining the situation once, and when I got to the part about how some women would kill to have my girlish long legs, the guy just stared at me in disbelief and said, "You're holding up the line, sir."

Airport security has always been a big-time barometer for how famous you are and what for. The personnel will often key in on your face and take the time to briefly talk about a film or TV show they liked. Or hated. And it's all relative.

Because airport security is the great celebrity equalizer. Doesn't matter who you really are—it's who they THINK you are that matters.

I remember going through security with the late great director Ted Demme and Bruce Springsteen back in the nineties after some awards show in Los Angeles. Ted directed Bruce's celebrated music video for the song "Streets of Philadelphia," the theme from the Oscar-winning Jonathan Demme film *Philadelphia*.

The TSA staff was predominantly African American and, as I was being waved along, three of them erupted in smiles as they mentioned *Who's the Man?*, a 1993 hip-hop comedy flick starring Ed Lover, Dr. Dre, and every rap and hip-hop star of that era along with hot young comics like Bernie Mac, Bill Bellamy, etc., in which I'd done an extended cameo. The film had a big cult audience. I pointed out Ted, who directed it, and he became a little mini-celebrity for ninety seconds as they complimented him on his work and cleared him right through.

Which was when we noticed Bruce getting wanded. Being one of the world's most famous rock stars, Bruce had several rings, necklaces, bracelets, earrings, and chains adorning his body—and he had set off the metal detector multiple times. Right now he had his arms in the air and a look of consternation on his face.

"Hey, he's okay," Ted explained to the guard. "He's the Boss."

The woman with the wand was unimpressed. "He might be somebody's boss, but he sure ain't the boss of me," she retorted. "Turn around, Mr. Boss Man." As Bruce did so and smiled, she wanded him further.

"He's Bruce," Teddy said. "He's cool."

"It ain't cool to wear all this jewelry and whatnot and make my job harder, Mr. Bruce," she replied.

"Bruce SPRINGSTEEN," Teddy intoned. Which finally rang a celebrity bell that made her stop and stare.

And it dawned on me and Teddy—and the Boss—simultaneously: Bruce's demographic doesn't include a lot of black people. So that night at LAX, *Who's the Man?* trumped *Born in the U.S.A.* for one brief, shining moment. Proving once again, we're all just people.

Some of us who wear a lot of jewelry.

It's worth noting here that the first time I met Bruce was at a Tribeca restaurant in downtown Manhattan. A friend of mine was directing a movie and Bruce was considering doing the score for it. Walking in, I was greeted by Little Steven saying, "Denis, Steve Van Zandt. This is Bruce. Hey, let me ask you a question."

We were at one end of the empty bar, and my friend and a few other people were seated across the room deeply engaged in conversation.

Bruce had a sullen look on his face. Steven was very intense as he continued with, "You call up your best friend and invite him to a wedding; you leave him a nice message. Now this is a guy you've known your whole friggin' life—and instead of callin' you back to say yes I'm comin' or no I can't make it, the guy has his ASSISTANT call. Not him—his assistant. Now I ask you: Is that or is that not a bullshit move, right?"

So there I stood, with Bruce and Little Steven staring back at me—two rock icons awaiting my response. One so famous that just the mention of his first name was enough to identify him anywhere in the world (except sometimes at airport security). The other one so notable, his nickname was all he needed wherever he went (except, I'm assuming, at airport security, where they might mistake him for a pirate).

But in this very moment, the power of fame was being called into question and weighed against regular guy friendship and common working-class courtesy.

I was still fairly new to fame at the time, but smart enough to know that in the celebrity pecking order, Bruce outranked Steven and Steven outranked me. So just like in the army, I wasn't gonna fuck with our commanding officer.

Even though Lieutenant Van Zandt was supposedly talking in abstract terms, it was clear that General Springsteen was the aim of his ire. Now personally, in my brief reign in Fameland, I'd already had some run-ins with old friends and family members over wedding invites and birthday bashes I couldn't attend, often responding through my assistant because my schedule was so insane. Thus my very diplomatic answer:

"Perhaps, Steve, this best friend of yours is extremely busy and didn't want to keep you waiting. What's the difference really if it's his assistant or his wife calling you back, as long as someone makes sure you know what you need to know. By the way, if this best friend is coming, isn't that the most important part of the equation?"

I almost didn't believe my own improvisational bullshit on that one, but it worked: Steve did what we would all come to know later on as one of his "Silvio Dante Talking to Tony Soprano Understanding Nods," turned to Bruce, turned back to me, and then said: "I never thought of it that way."

So the Boss and his best buddy clinked glasses and smiled at each other. *Holy shit*, I thought, *this Celebrity Expressway is sure full of unexpected potholes.*

Another time when I met Bruce was also fraught with bizarre energy. Long story short, Ted and I were asked to develop an original angle for a Rolling Stones concert film of their Voodoo Lounge Tour. Mick Jagger invited us to spend a few weeks watching the Stones rehearse and then attend the first couple of stadium gigs, shoot some backstage stuff, and get to know everyone in the band. Which was exhilarating. Especially when seconds after meeting Keith and Ron Wood, they started asking me questions about "The Asshole Song."

And then started singing the chorus. That remains a career high point for me.

All you need to know about the Stones is this: the real reason they are so great is because of how hard they work. Every day at every rehearsal they went all out with 150% high-energy musicianship. And then later, back at the hotel over drinks and dinner, they would pepper us with questions about how they sounded, what we thought of the set list, and were there any old songs we missed and thought might work better in the show.

Jagger was a gem—one of the most charming, smart, dynamic, and funny people I've ever met. Period. I brought my brother down to hang out for a couple of days and Mick ended up fetching him a Heineken one night while asking what his favorite tunes were and why. I can still see the shock on my brother's face as Mick handed him a cold beer and waited for his opinion on "Jumpin' Jack Flash."

Keith was a tough cookie and the genuine musical director. There's a reason almost every Stones song kicks off with his riff ringing out first—and he doesn't miss a detail onstage or off. Plus, he had a great laugh. As did Ronnie. Charlie was always the quiet guy with a sly smile and a polite hello every morning. The entire experience was like a dream. Mick and Keith made sure we got tickets for all of our friends and family members before we'd even considered asking. They were true gentlemen.

Now, during this run the MTV Video Music Awards were held in New York City and both Bruce and the Stones were nominated and playing the show. I presented an award that night, and afterward Teddy and I were hanging out backstage when the Stones finished playing. In the wings, Mick invited us to their private after-party. Which of course we said yes to.

As Mick walked away, Teddy whispered out of the side of his mouth: "Don't tell Bruce we're going to the Stones party."

"What? Whadda you—"

"Shhh. I told Bruce we would go to his party but I'd rather go to the Stones', so just follow my lead."

Half a second later, there was the Boss.

"Great job, man!" Teddy said.

"Amazing, Bruce, just—amazing!" I chimed in.

"Thanks, guys. So I'll see you later at the hotel?"

This was when Teddy panicked: "Um, well—it turns out—uhh—Denis has a thing."

This was when I panicked. My eyes almost fell out of my head. Because Bruce's eyes were looking right into them:

"Oh. You're having a party too?"

"No, it's—not a party. It's—more like—like a thing."

Bruce seemed puzzled:

"What kind of thing?"

I looked at Teddy, seeking some kind of help. He didn't offer any. The fucker. So I said: "It's just a, um, like a—you know what it is? It's—a dinner. A dinner thing."

"Oh. Well, why don't you guys come by after the dinner?"

Still no help from Teddy. He waited for me to nervously answer with this improvisational genius: "Yeah, well it's not just a dinner, it's a, um—dinner PARTY kind of thing. It's a—benefit, actually."

Don't ask me why I said "benefit." Maybe because it sounded more official? Which it did. For about two seconds.

"Nice. What's the charity?"

This was the next great idea to fly out of my Lying Rolodex: "Cancer. Musicians with cancer."

"Oh. That's cool. What's the name of it?"

Here I turned the tables on Teddy. "What's the name of it again, Teddy?"

And he turned them right back on me. "I dunno. It's your event. Not mine. I'm just going to support a great cause."

Then there was a long and awkward beat of silence. I guess Bruce was waiting for me to come up with the name. Which I was desperately asking my brain to create. Which it didn't. So Bruce gave me a suspicious look and said:

"Okay. Well, good luck with that. Teddy, I'll see you next week in L.A. Have a good night, boys."

And away he went. There was another awkward pause as we both stood there with frozen smiles on our faces until Bruce was safely out of earshot. Then I said: "You think he bought it?"

"A fucking cancer dinner party benefit THING? With no name? Who the fuck would buy THAT?"

Needless to say, we went to the Stones party. Which the Stones weren't at. But I did come up with a great name for my imaginary event: Tunes Against Tumors. I know, it sucks. Teddy thought so, too.

And you can bet your ass the Boss wouldn't have bought it.

I ran into Mick Jagger a few more times over the years and he not only always remembered me but remained his very charismatic self. And I saw Keith again about eight years later in the strangest of circumstances.

While on vacation in the Caribbean with my wife and a few other couples, I went down to the beach solo early one morning to catch some rays and enjoy the peaceful view. It was absolutely empty. Just me and the birds. When off in the distant waves, something caught my eye.

Slowly emerging from the water, a human head. Like Martin Sheen in *Apocalypse Now*.

Inch by inch. Black hair. Then open eyes. Followed by a weathered face. Then the rest of a very tan and slender man. In a pair of denim shorts. And what looked like an unbuttoned woman's blouse, open to the navel and tied off just above his waist.

Within a few seconds I realized: it was Keith Fucking Richards. Appearing out of the ocean as if I'd conjured his spirit. Vaguely humming some song, lost in thought, he sauntered up the beach, looked at me, and said: "Hey, man. How YOU doin'?"

"Hey, Keith—I'm doin' great. You?"

"Fuckin' great. You got a smoke?"

I said yeah and offered him a cigarette and my lighter. He lit up, inhaled, exhaled, and threw his head back, surveying our gorgeous surroundings. Then he said: "Fantastic day, eh?"

"Yes. Yes, it is."

Then he handed me the lighter and started walking away. "Awright, mate. Catch you later."

And that was it. It's probably the most major rock star move I've ever witnessed—emerging out of a warm teal ocean for a brief chat and smoke and then calmly disappearing over a breezy white sand dune. Like an apparition. Fantastic day indeed.

But he wasn't an apparition. Because two nights later I walked into the empty hotel beach bar, which was essentially a fancy straw hut. There sat Keith. Still barefoot. In the exact same outfit. But somehow looking fresh as a daisy. Eyes brighter than diamonds. He was sipping a drink when he saw me and nonchalantly said, "Hey, kid—you got another smoke?" as if we had just seen each other two minutes ago.

I said sure and handed him one. Which he lit up and exhaled.

Then he offered this: "I saw a pod of dolphins today. Stunning sight." Took two more languorous hits off the cigarette, smiled a glowing smile, and said, "You know what's funny? Mick Jagger getting the bloody MBE from the Queen. Sir Mick Fucking Jagger." He threw his wild hairy head back with a deep, riotous laugh that lasted a full five seconds.

Then there was a strange moment of awkward silence as he stared at the floor, humming some vague musical phrase.

After a few more seconds of silence, he finished his drink, stood up in all his tan glory to say, "Awright—see ya round, kid!" and gracefully stepped out the door, taking an elegant turn into a lush tropical garden full of colorful bushes and towering plants. Within a heartbeat he had evaporated in the darkness, leaving behind a hush of whispering leaves.

I stared at the bartender for a second. Both of us smiled in amazement.

Then I said, "Give me two of whatever he was having."

About five years later, I was at a friend's birthday barbecue when I wandered off toward the tennis court, where a couple of people were whacking the ball around. I was watching them for a few seconds when I heard: "Hey, man, can you go find me an ashtray?"

I turned to see Keith, seated and coloring a unicorn in a kid's coloring book. I am NOT shitting you. As I gathered in this visual, Keith said: "I need an ashtray and a hot pink crayon."

I didn't know what to say, but this seemed appropriate: "A hot pink crayon?"

"For the mane. I'm doing the body in Blizzard Blue, the tail's gonna be Electric Lime—I think Hot Pink would be perfect for the mane. Or Purple Pizzazz. Or Razzle-Dazzle Rose. Any of those shades would do. And an ashtray."

Again, not sure of what to say, I blurted out: "Okay. I'll check in the house."

So off I went. Searching for fluorescent-colored crayons. For at least half an hour. In the kitchen, in the living room, in the basement—asking a bevy of people where I might find them. Including some kids I came across in a playroom, who I had to yell at because they weren't paying attention.

"Hey, guys! Stop running around for a second and listen to me! I need your help here! Now shut up and listen for a minute!"

Needless to say, they were a little shocked. Thinking they had done something wrong. So I tried to calm them down with a fun smile and this offering: "You guys ever seen *The Sandlot*?"

That's a baseball movie I made in 1993 that became a big hit with kids of all ages. And it's still a favorite almost twenty-five years later. Several of these kids had seen it and answered yes. I smiled even bigger and charmingly explained who I was: "Well, I played the stepdad in that movie."

"No you didn't," a little girl immediately said.

"Yes I did," I replied sweetly.

"You're too old," another girl piped in.

"And wrinkly!" some wiseass boy said, which got a huuuge laugh and a couple of: "Look at his wrinkles!" Plus this: "His face is melting!" Which got a massive laugh. MASSIVE.

They started chiming in on top of each other in a chorus of laughter and finger pointing: "His face is melting, his face is melting!" They laughed and snickered and cackled.

Until I snapped:

"Goddammit, I really WAS the stepdad in *Sandlot* and I need a HOT PINK FUCKING CRAYON and I need it RIGHT FUCKING NOW!" I shouted. "And if you wanna see someone with a wrinkly melting face then come outside and see the guy I'm tryna find the fucking crayon for!"

The kids looked up at me in total confusion. A couple of them seemed to be on the verge of tears. I didn't care anymore. But I knew I was going to have to apologize.

That's when the wiseass reached into a box of crayons and pulled out a Hot Magenta. Which looked pretty fucking pink to me. Plus, when I asked him if Hot Magenta was close to Razzle-Dazzle Rose, he said, "Calm down, mister. You're very sweaty."

Fucking kids. I left in a huff. Without saying sorry.

Grabbing an ashtray on my way out the kitchen door, I ran like Usain Bolt over to the tennis courts to find Keith.

Who was gone. As in GONE gone.

No coloring book, no crayons, no cigarette butts.

I searched the grounds of the property. For a long time. No sign of him. I started wondering if he was pissed at me. Then I started wondering if I had actually seen him at all. I went into the bathroom to take a piss and splash some water on my sweaty, wrinkly, melting candle of a face. What the fuck?

Later on, as the birthday boy opened presents, I saw him unroll a gently wrapped tube of paper with a ribbon around it: a neon-blue unicorn with a bright lime-green tail and mane. Signed by Keith Richards.

So it hadn't been some kind of fever dream after all.

I haven't seen Keith since, but it wouldn't surprise me at all if I bumped into him five years from now in the strangest of circumstances and he said, "Hey, man—where's that fucking ash-tray I asked you for?"

Cigarettes have often led to strange celebrity kinships for me.

Like the one and only time I ever had the privilege to meet one of my all-time heroes, David Bowie.

It was early in my career, just after I'd gotten big. We were both booked to appear on an English TV show and I'd heard from two old comedian friends of mine—the brilliant Steven Wright and Bobcat Goldthwaite—that Bowie was a big comedy fan. They'd both had the opportunity to meet David after he'd seen them perform as they shot to fame in the early eighties. So I naturally assumed he'd be a fan of mine. Plus, I knew he smoked. When I got to the theater the stage manager explained that in order to smoke, you had to step out a back door.

In the lead-up to doing the show I'd imagined what my conversation with Bowie would be like. Something along these lines:

BOWIE
Denis! How are you? I've been sooo looking forward to meeting you. You're soooo funny! You're absolutely my favorite comedian.

ME
Oh, thank you, David, that's awesome, man. But listen—YOU are my favorite rock star of all time; I mean, you bridged the gap for me when I was a teenager.

BOWIE
What gap was that?

ME

When shitty prog rock and folky "singer/songwriter" pussies took over—like Seals and Crofts and Loggins and Messina.

BOWIE

I absolutely *HATED* those assholes. Which reminds me— "The Asshole Song" is genius. Just genius. Let's sing it tonight.

ME

Sing it where?

BOWIE

On the show.

ME

What show?

BOWIE

THIS show.

ME

You mean, like—in two hours?

BOWIE

Yes, in two hours. I had the band rehearse it once I found out you were going to be on. We've got it down, man.

ME

But—

BOWIE

I won't take no for an answer. I've already arranged it with the producer and I've learned all the harmonies as well.

ME

I—I don't know what to say.

BOWIE

I'll take that as a yes. Plus, I want you to have dinner with us after the show—then come to the studio. Me and the band are gonna be jamming tonight and I wanna write a comedy tune. I've never really written one and this would be the perfect opportunity. You and me as writing partners, mate.

ME

Oh, wow. Okay! I'm in.

BOWIE

Listen—I've also got some copies of *The Ref* and *No Cure for Cancer* in my dressing room. Would you mind signing them for me?

ME

Of course not.

Pretty awesome, right? Now here's how it really went. I stepped out into the alley and lit up a smoke when:

BOWIE

Pardon me. Would you have a light?

ME

(*very excited*)

Yes. Yes. I'm Denis, by the way.

BOWIE

Hello, Denis, I'm David.

ME
(still excited)
I know. I'm like—your biggest fan. I'm like—a huuuge fan.

BOWIE
Oh. Well, thank you.

ME
(trying to calm down)
I'm the comedian. Denis Leary?

BOWIE
Oh. Nice. I love stand-up comedy. Where are you from,
New York?

ME
(slightly calmer)
Boston. I'm mostly in L.A. now because my career is really
taking—

BOWIE
Boston. Do you know Steven Wright?

ME
(making a connection)
Oh yeah. I went to college with Steven Wright. He and I—

BOWIE
Omigod. What's he like? I mean, I've met him—
I'm like HIS biggest fan. But I didn't really get to
KNOW him per se. Is he always that shy? Or is it
just a persona?

ME
(*why isn't this about me?*)
Um, yeah. He's shy. I'm normally a little shy too, even though
my persona is the exact opp—

BOWIE
He's a genius. Truly one of a kind. What about Bobcat
Goldthwaite? I've met him as well. God, I'm such a huuuge
fan of his. Did he always do that sort of punk rock comedy
character? It's very original.

ME
(*fuck Bobcat Goldthwaite*)
Totally, yeah. Speaking of original, can I tell you that "Jean
Genie" was—

CREW MEMBER
David, they're ready for sound check now.

BOWIE
(*to Crew Member*)
Oh, thank you very much.
(*to me, as he exits*)
Nice to meet you, Kevin.

And—The End.

David walked away and I stood exhaling smoke. I saw him onstage that night but never again met him in person. It wasn't
the first time I was identified as an anonymous Kevin. But it
was close to being the last. I got very famous within a year of
my singular Bowie experience. And pretty soon the only Kevin
I'd be confused with was already a movie star. I was about to

become living proof that fame is not only fleeting, it often moves so fucking fast that within the course of a single conversation I could become several different people. And sometimes even manage to change gender, which is considered pretty cool these days. My next book? *Erasing My Balls* by Dr. Denis Leary.

I love being famous.
It's almost like being
white.

—CHRIS ROCK

ALL TALL SKINNY FAMOUS WHITE GUYS LOOK ALIKE

I used to have this showbiz dream that years after our encounter, Bowie would be sitting on a couch watching *Mystic River* when he'd point to Kevin Bacon on-screen and tell Iman, "Hey, I met that guy backstage in London once before he was famous."

Kevin Bacon is low on my doppelgänger list, but he does pop up from time to time. Almost always in airports. And when this happens, it usually involves a lot of passion on the part of his fans. And I guess because they are so passionate, I always feel it's important to explain why I'm not him. Which then takes at least five minutes because they say things like, "Okay, we get it— you're trying to keep a low profile. Can you take a quick photo?" and "Tell Kyra we love her!"

So at a certain point I just stopped arguing and gave in. I'd sign Kevin's name and pose for a pic and promise to tell Kyra. Which took way less time and never came back to bite me in the ass.

Until the summer of 2016.

I jumped into an Uber vehicle in Manhattan, heading about twenty blocks to my apartment. Nice SUV, comfortable air-conditioning, and some Frank Ocean playing on the stereo system. Calm, cool, and relaxed. After the normal hellos and man-is-it-hot-outside patter between the driver and me, there was a moment of silence as we traveled along listening to the music.

Then I noticed the driver glancing at me in the rearview mirror. As we came to a red light and the car stopped moving, he did a full prairie dog on me—straightening his spine as he rose up four inches higher in the seat and momentarily froze in place: eyes wide with alert and locked on me in the mirror with full recognition. Like a meerkat spotting some dinner.

"Footloose," he said.

"I'm sorry?"

"Footloose—you the *Footloose* man!"

Ah shit, I thought, *another Kevin Bacon fan.*

"My wife, she love that movie! I love movie too! You a great dancer, Kevin Bacon! I gotta take picture for my wife!"

As he fumbled for his phone, I thought about owning up and telling him I wasn't Kevin. But the light was about to change and he seemed so excited and happy—plus, there wasn't any traffic and it was less than ten minutes until he'd be dropping me off, so I made a split-second decision:

"Did your wife like *Mystic River*?"

"The murder one with Sean Penn? Crazy good! We see everything you in—but we like the *Footloose* the best."

And now he leaned across the center console, held his phone at arm's length, and smiled. I did the same, put my arm around his shoulder, and CLICK CLICK CLICK he took three fast photos.

"Thank you, Kevin Bacon—my wife go crazy."

Then the light changed and we were on our way again. I'd crossed a line now, and there was no going back. So: "Did you watch my TV show *The Following*?"

"Omigod, yes—soooo scary. Very scary. And we watch your wife on *her* show. Your wife a great actress. My wife love your wife. She *The Closer*! Ha ha!"

"Yes, she is. Yup. I'm a lucky guy."

"My name is Manny."

"Nice to meet you, Manny."

"Nice to meet YOU, Kevin Bacon."

Manny had a smile bursting wide across his face. Total joy: "You do all the dancing in the *Footloose*?"

"Oh yeah. Every single step."

"You a wonderful dancer."

"Thank you."

"Wait until I tell my wife. She won't believe this happen."

"Well, you have the pictures to prove it."

"Yes. Yes, I do."

I knew the pictures would probably be a disappointment. His wife was likely to look at them, feel an itch of doubt, and then Google Kevin Bacon, coming to the sudden realization that the man in Manny's Uber was in fact an impostor. But that scene would take place hours from now when I was safely ensconced at home—never having to deal with the deception. I sat back and enjoyed the summery New York City sights. Six more minutes to home. When I heard Manny say this:

"He's right here in the backseat, honey! Wait, hold on—Kevin, my wife on the phone. She don't believe Kevin Bacon is in my car. Say hello to her. Her name is Maru."

And with that, he handed me the phone. Shit. No turning back now:

"Hello, Maru. This is Kevin Bacon." Maru went quiet.

"Maru? Are you there?"

"Yes. Hello, Kevin."

"Hi. How are you?"

"I like your movies."

"So I hear. Thank you."

"You're welcome. Is Kyra there?"

"Um, no. No she's not. She's at home."

"Oh—that's too bad. I love *The Closer*. When she won the Golden Globe and the Emmy I was so happy for her. She deserve it, too. She was the best in that show."

This kind of pissed me off. Maru was not only disappointed that Kyra Sedgwick wasn't also in Manny's Uber, but she was using her precious Kevin Bacon time to praise his absent wife's acting ability. Instead of my dancing. So I said this:

"You know I won a Golden Globe too, Maru."

"You did?"

"Yes. Best Dramatic Actor. For *Taking Chance*?"

"Oh. I didn't see that one. Was Kyra in it?"

"Nope. Just me. It's on HBO GO. Very good movie. Award-winning. Okay, nice talking to you, Maru."

"Tell Kyra I love her."

"I will. Here's Manny."

And with that I handed Manny his phone. Stewing a little about the fact that even while pretending to be another famous actor, my fake award-winning talent gets overshadowed by the abilities of my also-famous fake show business wife.

This is why things never would have worked out between Kyra and me.

Her success and multiple major awards would have been a sticking point for my jealousy. Not to mention the fact that *The Closer* ran for seven highly acclaimed seasons, while *The Following* was canceled after a critically panned two. My overinflated ego and underlying insecurities would have ruined our relationship.

But then I suddenly realized what a great guy Kevin Bacon was—so supportive of his wife. And I remembered how in love they seemed whenever they walked a red carpet together. They'd been happily married for almost thirty years. Plus, Kevin was apparently a great father. I changed my mind. You know what? It was an honor to be mistaken for such a wonderful man. That's when the SUV pulled over to the curb and I heard this:

"Hey, what the hell, dude?"

Manny was parked and furious. He held up his phone. On it was a Google image of the actual Kevin Bacon. Suddenly looking very unlike me.

"Maru say you don't sound like Kevin Bacon and I say she crazy, but then I Google you up and Maru is right and now we know why—because you NOT HIM! Why you lie to me and my wife?"

Fuck. Fuck fuck fuck. I decided to come clean:

"Okay. I'm not Kevin Bacon. But I am a famous actor."

"Bullsheet."

"I'm Denis Leary."

"Danny who?"

Arrrgghh. This was now becoming insane.

"Maybe you don't know who I am but a lot of people—"

"You a liar! Cut the bullsheet and get the fuck out of my car before I call the cops! GET OUT! GET THE FUCK OUT! I GIVE YOU ZERO STARS!!!"

And there I stood. Caught in a lie I only told to make someone feel better. Walking the hot SoHo streets with sweaty pits and a shitty Uber rating, I went home, cranked the AC, and ordered in.

And watched *Footloose.*

Two things struck me: number one, I really don't look anything like Kevin Bacon. And number two, the dancing didn't look all that hard. Until I tried to mimic some of the moves.

And pulled a hamstring.

I get the fact that a lot of tall Irish guys named Kevin, Denis, and Bryan can look alike, even to other white people. Not to mention Beyoncé. There are multiple guys named Kevin and Brian in my own family. Along with a bevy of Michaels and Johns on both sides of the ocean. And many of us are physically built the same. Even my sister Anne Marie looks a lot like me.

Which might explain this next story.

I was shooting an FX comedy series called *Sex&Drugs&Rock-&Roll* on the streets of New York City, playing a failed musician by the name of Johnny Rock. I had a shag haircut that could best be described as Rod Stewart meets Ziggy Stardust, and was sporting a very blousy rock star type of shirt, multiple necklaces and rings, plus a pair of very cool retro sunglasses—the kind Jackie Onassis wore back in the seventies.

A crowd had gathered to watch us film, and as the actress Elaine Hendrix and I finished a relationship argument, my character walked off down the block. Seconds after the director shouted cut, a female fan of mine broke through the barriers and ran up to breathlessly tell me, "I'm your biggest fan and I can't believe I'm seeing you, but I'm late for a meeting and can't hang around—could you just take one quick photo with me?" I said, "Of course I can! Anything for my biggest fan!" So she whipped out her phone, I leaned in close to her and smiled broadly as she CLICK CLICK CLICKED, and then she beamed: "Thank you so much! I wish I could stay longer! *Glee* is my favorite show and YOU are my favorite character! BYE!"

As she rushed away waving, I waved back—realizing she thought I was Jane Fucking Lynch. Which had to be impossible. But I turned toward a plate-glass store window a few feet away and took a gander at myself. Holy shit. I did look like Jane Lynch. In Jane's defense, a much manlier and far less pretty Jane Lynch. Really more like Jane Lynch's much older and weather-beaten brother.

This happened a lot while I was shooting *Sex&Drugs&Rock& Roll*—the common denominator being the days I was wearing a blousy shirt. Because whenever I was out in public dressed as Johnny but sporting a tight-fitting T-shirt, I wasn't Jane Lynch anymore. I somehow became Jon Bon Jovi.

My costars included a trio of celebrity head-turners. Liz Gillies and Elaine Hendrix were gorgeous to begin with but also well known for iconic roles they had played. Teenage girls would go insane when they saw Jade from the hit Nickelodeon show *Victorious* walking the streets of New York, and surround Liz, begging her for an autograph. Women in their twenties would freak out when they saw Elaine because her character in *The Parent Trap* was one of their all-time childhood favorites. Plus, everywhere we went, women of all ages would scream "AIDAN!" at John Corbett, still enamored of Sarah Jessica's dreamy boyfriend from *Sex and the City*.

During production of our first season, a girl approached me on set and—for the only time in my career—ran the full famous-guy gamut on me in one fell swoop. We were shooting on a busy street in Brooklyn and taking a break as the camera guys got ready to roll. So Elaine, Liz, and I were just standing outside a café chatting away when we noticed a woman in her thirties walk by twice, staring at us each time.

On her third pass, she sidled shyly up to me and quietly said, "Excuse me, can I ask you a question?" She had an interesting accent so I answered: "Yes. I love your accent, by the way. Do you mind if I ask where you're from?"

"I'm from Belgium."

"Cool. I've been to Brussels. Loved it."

She got even quieter now: "Are you—him?"

Glad to be recognized by one of my European fans, I said, "Yup."

This she said very loudly: "Jon Bon Jovi! I knew it!"

Elaine and Liz burst into gales of laughter. "He's not Jon Bon Jovi," Elaine explained.

"Yes he is."

"Nope—he's not," Elaine replied.

"He is somebody famous though," Liz Gillies added.

"A famous actor," Elaine clued.

The girl looked me up and down again. Then seemed to get it: "Yes. Okay. Wait. Yes. You're a very good actor. I've seen you in many films. I know who you are."

Elaine said, "Willem Dafoe?"

And the girl went: "YES! THAT'S IT! Can I take a picture?"

"He's not Willem Dafoe," Liz explained.

This stopped her in her tracks. She narrowed her eyes. Once more gave me the full up and down, then hopefully asked: "Kevin Bacon?"

"No. I'm sorry. I'm not."

"He's Denis Leary," Liz said.

She went silent for a second. Then it all dawned on her: "Ohhhh. Okay. Right. Now I see it. My mom loves you." She looked a little deflated. And ready to move on. "Okay. Nice to meet you," she said as she walked away.

"You don't wanna take a picture?" I implored.

"No, no. That's okay. Thank you!"

And off she went. Leaving all of us laughing in her wake.

It's not every celebrity that can bring such disappointment on an international basis. As well as all over America.

Once I was shooting a football movie called *Draft Day* in Cleveland, Ohio. My character had very short hair and often wore a sport coat and dressy pants. Which is the outfit I had on one morning as I came out the front door of the hotel and noticed a lot of lesbians.

I'm sure the last five words of that sentence will be considered sexist or genderist or judgy by recently hired Sensitive Readers, but I'm telling you there is no other way to describe it: I was surrounded by lesbians. Lesbians in small chatty circles. Lines of lesbians getting some kind of credentials from a table full of lesbians. And a stream of other lesbians coming out of several luxury lesbian buses and jumbo lesbo passenger vans. I had no idea what the hell was going on. Until I heard this:

"Ellen! Omigod! Are you here for the convention?"

This woman thought I was Ellen DeGeneres. Attending the Cleveland Pride weekend. And the woman who singled me out was part of an Ohio lesbian delegation who had meetings and events planned at my hotel, along with a full three days of other celebrations. A couple of her friends lasered in on me too:

"Hey—Ellen DeGeneres is here!"

"Are you marching in the parade? Where's Portia?"

Now, I know as some men get older, we start to look like aging lesbians. There's nothing we can do about that except maybe plastic surgery. Which I'm never doing. This is my face. For better or worse. Mostly worse from here on out. And I don't have a problem with that. What I do have a problem with is this: Ellen has much better skin than me, far fewer wrinkles, and way more feminine eyes.

Fortunately, the majority of women around me that morning agreed with my summation.

"That's not Ellen."

"He's a guy, for chrissakes."

"You are somebody, though. Who are you?"

"Denis Leary."

"No you're not. Denis Leary has much longer hair."

Such is life.

I only get mistaken for Ellen once every five years or so. But every single time, my hair IS short. And I have on a T-shirt and pants with a sport coat. Hey, I'm not stereotyping here. I'm the VICTIM of a stereotype. But I have to say—the level of excitement and animated joy that springs from Ellen's fans when they think I might be her?

Makes me a very willing one.

Now, just as a form of review, let's make an official list:

PEOPLE DENIS LEARY IS MOST OFTEN MISTAKEN FOR:
1. Willem Dafoe (all the time, anywhere)
2. Bryan Adams (by some people, but especially Beyoncé)
3. Bon Jovi (if I sport a T-shirt, shag haircut, and jewelry)
4. Jane Lynch (with shag haircut, blousy shirt, and jewelry)
5. Ellen DeGeneres (with short haircut, T-shirt, no jewelry)
6. Kevin Bacon (only in airports, Belgium, or by Uber drivers)
7. Christopher Walken (once, by an Hispanic security guard)

Let me explain number seven. I was working at an editing facility in New York City a couple of years ago and headed out for a smoke when I stopped to tell the security guard, "Hey, I'm just gonna have a quick cigarette and come back in, but I forgot my pass card."

"No problem, I won't forget YOU, Mr. Walken."

I said thanks and ambled outside, a bit distracted by the project we were working on upstairs, when it hit me: that guy thinks I'm Christopher Walken? Chris Walken is a friend of mine. Chris Walken is a talented guy. Chris Walken is an Oscar-winning actor. AND FOURTEEN YEARS OLDER THAN ME!

I glanced at myself in the building's front door glass: no way I looked that old. I didn't wanna get into an argument with the guy. Or ask someone passing by on the sidewalk who they thought I was. But I also didn't wanna be Chris Walken to this security guard for the next three weeks while I was coming in and out of his building.

So I Googled *Suicide Kings,* a culty heist movie Chris and I did back in the late nineties. He played a kidnapped mob boss and I was his devoted right-hand man on a mad search to find him. Voilà! First image up was Chris and I standing side by side, leaning on the hood of a car and staring straight into the camera. I had extremely close-cropped short hair and rock-star-cool sunglasses on—and looked a lot younger than Chris. So on my way back in I stopped at the front desk and proudly showed this photo to the security guy. Pointed to my image. And smiled. He was very impressed:

"Holy shit—when did you do a movie with Sting?"

Suffice to say it took fifteen minutes and another twenty-five Google photos for me to prove who I actually was. And you know what finally did the deed? My voice. His kids were huge fans of Diego from the *Ice Age* movies. Thank God.

Side note to Kellyanne Conway: If you're bummed out about people saying you and I resemble each other, do yourself a favor: don't cut the hair.

The one and only time I prayed to be mistaken for some other celebrity happened two summers ago.

I was driving back from Detroit.

Let me start by saying: I drive everywhere. I love seeing this great country of ours from ground level. I also love playing my favorite music very loud. On big truck speakers. And I only drive trucks. Whether it's a large SUV or a pick up. Why? Because I can. Do they eat gas and cause climate change? You bet your ass they do. Listen, build me a truck that travels on chia seeds and I'll be the first guy in line to buy it. Until then: Fuck you. Call Sting and set up another rain forest benefit.

So I'm driving back from Detroit.

And despite what you're about to read, just like most Americans I usually use the state-run rest stops when I have to go to the bathroom. But this one particular morning I miscalculated.

I had been visiting some Detroit Fire Department friends of mine for a Leary Firefighters Foundation charity presentation, and doing some local media to drum up funding. Now, I'm a worst-case-scenario type of guy. What I like to call an optimistic pessimist. I always expect the absolute baddest possible thing to happen, and I look forward to getting it over with. It's an approach that has served me well.

Think about it: I'm the son of Irish immigrants, raised in Massachusetts. When I was six years old they assassinated our Boston-born, first-ever Irish president, and when I was ten our baseball team, the Red Sox, lost the World Series under a cloud of ill will that during decades of subsequent near-misses would become known as the Curse of the Bambino. Lesson learned: if you got your hopes up too high, someone was bound to crush them like a bug.

So I'm driving. Back from Detroit.

I'd eaten a big breakfast at the hotel that morning and, just as I left the room, grabbed a roll of toilet paper and threw it into my gym bag. Why? Because JFK got his head blown off, that's why. Because of Bill Buckner and 1986. Don't know what that refers to? Google the misery. Which is over now because the Red Sox have won three World Series championships. In less than ten years! Talk about hope and change.

So. Driving. Detroit. Me.

Listening to some old Motown hits. Very, very loud. About an hour or so outside the city. When my colon sends a message: we have to take a crap. Okay. Should have gone before I left the hotel but not an immediate problem. I can hold it for at least another ten minutes. Wait until the next rest stop. I've done it a million times. We all have. Two more songs and a public toilet. Perfect timing.

Marvin Gaye on the mix. Moving along at a cool 95 mph when I see a highway sign ahead. I can tell it's a NEXT REST STOP sign, so I'm feeling pretty good. Until I get a little closer. Close enough to read the entire thing. Now I don't remember exactly what the sign said, but I do recall the gist of it: NEXT REST STOP—YOU SHOULD HAVE WORN A DIAPER. It was some crazy number like thirty-six miles. In other words: an entire album away!

I cinched up my sphincter as tight as I could but it was a losing proposition. We've all been there: that moment in time when you suddenly realize you have no more butt-muscle control. Plus, you're in a seated position so as far as your anus is concerned it's already Go Time. My colon was sending me emergency signals. Cramping up. If my ass was on Twitter this tweet would've been hashtagged HaveToTakeItNow.

No exits in sight. No exits listed on the GPS until AFTER the next rest stop. And thirty-five miles to go. I had no other option. So I picked a leafy, green area with a nice chunk of woods and an already trodden path coming out of it. As if quite a few other people had pulled over and walked into it to take a piss. So I cleverly parked in front of that path. Knowing the big Ford F-150 would block me from anyone's view while I went about my business.

Which it did.

I know because in the precious little time between me exiting the truck and the crap exiting my colon, I focused in on what was in front of me. The last thing I wanted was to be in a squatting position with my pants around my ankles when a state trooper showed up. But now my ass made it clear: bombs away. I had maybe two seconds until release. So there I was, roll of toilet paper in one hand, belt buckle in the other, as my pants fell around my ankles, and I squatted down: BAM.

It was over that fast.

What the hell? I don't think I ever took that quick a shit in my life. One bend and I was done. And I mean DONE done. Nothing left inside. And my colon felt cleansed. For years Jimmy Kimmel and Howard Stern had been talking about how great the Squatty Potty is and Squatty Potty This and Squatty Potty That. Those two could talk for hours about how the squat position was healthier, more natural, and better for your entire digestive system. They even talked about Squatty Potty on Howard's radio show. It's a wood footrest you place next to the toilet that forces your body into a more beneficial bathroom position. I always thought they were out of their minds. Until I was standing in these Michigan woods staring down at what was quite possibly the most perfect poop I'd ever taken. And then I realized: Howard and Jimmy were geniuses. I barely had to wipe! Which was when I heard, "HEY, MAN! WHAT THE FUCK!"

I looked up to see a fence. And just inside that fence, about forty horrified people at a cookout. And their kids! That's when it dawned on this thick Irish skull: I'd never looked behind me. I certainly thought I'd glanced deeper into the woods on my way in, but really I was so concerned about someone seeing me from the highway side that the last few yards of entry had been spent facing forward. Just like the forty people staring at me right now. And their kids!

So I did what you would have done.

I pulled up my pants and ran like a bat out of hell, tossing the roll of toilet paper into the bushes. It sounded like a couple of angry fathers jumped the fence and were headed up the path in chase because I heard a few more "HEYs!" that seemed to be getting closer as I jumped into my truck and peeled away. Want to know how fast a Ford pickup goes from zero to eighty miles per hour? Here's the answer: pretty fucking fast. And the whole time I was praying, *Please let them think it was Willem Dafoe. Or Jon Bon Jovi. Anyone but me.*

Twenty-five years after gaining notoriety, I'm speeding down a Michigan highway hoping people don't remember me at all.

Which is perfect. For so many reasons.

When my MTV rants and hit one-man show *No Cure for Cancer* first caught fire back in 1992, I was considered the Next Big Thing. Movie offers and magazine covers followed. And as my name got bigger, so did my ego. Which is where my wife comes in. She would cut me back down to size every time I got too full of myself, reminding me that I wasn't really a movie star—I was a father and a husband who happened to make movies for a living.

Because in the end, that's the only legacy anyone leaves behind: family. How you treated and loved your significant other bears a spiritual witness even after you've departed. And if you have children, how they are raised speaks an enduring volume about your moral backbone and beliefs. As do your closest friends and relatives. Charity also counts: *To whom much is given, much is expected in return.* I picked that nugget up from my parents. My mom's proud that I'm successful, but far prouder of what I might have accomplished as a dad. And how I use my fame for lending a helping hand to people less fortunate than we are.

My parents should have honorary doctorates. Dr. John Leary was a devoted father who taught me a strong work ethic and how to judge people by character instead of skin color. Dr. Nora Leary taught me family values, good citizenship, and how housewives like her actually created feminism. By empowering their daughters on a daily basis. My wife, Dr. Ann Leary, showed me how important my kids are and the proper place for all the Hollywood bullshit.

But just like my friend Dr. Lenny Clarke, first I had to learn how to listen. I'm doing a lot of good deeds now to make up for all the idiotic behavior I perpetrated earlier on. So I glommed onto this cold, hard fact: Fame is not forever. It is forever ephemeral. Each celebrity name and face is a cotton candy idea that brings a sugary smile or breathy swoon for several years or so, but eventually melts away into empty-calorie oblivion.

Think about it.

These days, if you mention a handsome movie star with debonair comic ability and the last name Grant, most people think of Hugh. Not Cary.

Remember Paul Newman? My kids thought he was a chef. Because his smiling face adorned every bottle of salad dressing and each microwave popcorn bag they ingested for the first fifteen years of their lives. Until we force-fed them *Butch Cassidy and the Sundance Kid* one summer evening. And then they wondered who the blond guy was. And what the fuss was all about. But once Robert Redford appeared opposite Chris Evans in *Captain America,* THEN they thought he was cool.

An entire generation of kids don't know who Johnny Carson was, never mind almost every single guest who ever appeared on his show. My nieces and nephews think of Goldie Hawn as Kate Hudson's mother. Seventies box-office king Burt Reynolds is now known as the Old Guy from *Boogie Nights,* and John Wayne is recognized as the first two names of a famed murderous clown called Gacy.

Serial killers are much more likely to be remembered than cinematic stars.

Such is the nature of the insatiable fame beast.

A very precious few entertainers get chosen to light up the sky for posterity. Mostly musicians, which I think has to do with the power of a three-minute miracle—a memorable song that makes your feet move or your heart glow while imbuing the soul with longing and inspiration. Frank Sinatra and the Rolling Stones, Louie Armstrong and Janis Joplin, Judy Garland and David Bowie, are all artists my kids came to know on their own. Not to mention Tony Bennett and the Beatles. The song "White Christmas" may be the only connection this generation has with Bing Crosby, but that holiday number will keep his name on American lips until time stands still.

Nick Lowe? Nope. The Replacements? Not a chance. For millennials, Iggy Pop might have started out as the guy who sang "Search and Destroy" on an Audi commercial and the Clash as the band behind the Choice Hotels tune "Should I Stay or Should I Go." But that brief TV exposure leads to downloads of their other music and makes them legendary all over again.

It doesn't work that way for old TV shows and their stars, though. *Columbo* is mourned as a favorite brand of yogurt that left the dairy shelves in 2010, instead of the magnificent show starring Peter Falk, who died a year later. Remember *Hill Street Blues*? Congratulations. Nobody under fifty does.

Quick, name the star of that show . . .

I couldn't do it either. Had to Google it just now. Answer? Daniel J. Travanti. Won two Emmys and a Golden Globe. A fine and talented actor still working in mostly anonymous TV guest shots at the age of seventy-seven—just one example of how fleeting the bright spotlight can be.

The Bob Hope Airport in Southern California recently changed its name to the Hollywood Burbank Airport because they needed bigger name recognition. Bob Hope wasn't a singer.

Dean Martin was a gifted artist with leading man looks who left behind a legacy that includes the biggest comedy box-office team of all time (with Jerry Lewis), many stunning dramatic film performances, and a hit TV show that ran for nine seasons. How is he remembered now?

As the guy who sang "Volare."

Prince's legacy will be "Purple Rain." The song. Not the movie.

And when it comes to the movies, you can count on two hands the classic old films—and the great actors who were lucky enough to star in them—that live on recognizably. Films like *The Godfather* give performers such as Pacino and Brando eternal illumination. *Goodfellas* and *Raging Bull* afford Bob De Niro and Joe Pesci infinite acclaim. Harrison Ford will be Han Solo in heaven, and Carrie Fisher's memory will never escape the embrace of the unforgettable Princess Leia. And the stars who died while still young, talented, and gorgeous? They remain James Dean, Heath Ledger, and Marilyn Monroe forevermore—frozen in time and our brain cells.

But for most of us other actors? We tend to be disposable.

Even if in 1994 your star was attached to a critically acclaimed cult comedy called *The Ref,* two decades later it leads to questions such as this: "Hey, what was the name of the lesbian-looking guy in that Christmas movie where he takes a crazy family hostage?"

I'm sure this conversation is happening in an airport somewhere in America right now as you read this:

> FAN
> Hey—are you Kevin Bacon?

> KEVIN BACON
> Yes I am.

> FAN
> Man, I loved you in *The Ref*!

Which is a far better conversation to hear than this one:

> FAN
> Kevin Bacon!

> KEVIN BACON
> Hey—how you doin'?

> FAN
> I saw you take a shit behind my cousin's house last summer!

The one guaranteed, inescapable form of infamy exists on the political world stage. Serve an asshole term or two in the White House or become the head dick of a dictatorially repressive evil government, and that ugly stench will stain your name for as long as this planet exists. And ruin things for everyone else in your family. Think about it: how many folks have you met with the last name Hitler? And have you ever met an Adolph? Or even a dog with that name? There's a reason you'll never study at the Joseph Goebbels Journalism School or fly Bin Laden Airlines.

It's a law of human nature that power can sometimes corrupt people. But absolute power? THAT is a guaranteed shit show.

Which is why we invented democracy.

Because we get to right the shit show when it finally hits the fan. Who knows what damage or good POTUS 45 may do in the next few years. If he turns things around and really does Make America Great Again, people will spend eternity posing for pictures on the solid gold Donald statue that Trump himself erects outside his D.C. hotel. But if he fucks it all up and gets ousted in 2020?

He'll still build the statue.

But the only posing on it will be done by pigeons. And angry voters giving his sculpted visage the finger.

There is no Richard Nixon statue in Washington, D.C. And there won't be a Nixon Airport.

Anywhere.

Ever.

And it's unlikely that we will see Hillary in a larger-than-life stone depiction.

But someday there will be a statue of America's first female president adorning a federal lawn or official edifice somewhere. As a matter of fact, we could use a lot more statues commemorating what women have done for this country. Abraham Lincoln's mom. George Washington's wife. Betty Fucking Ford. Who was instrumental in bringing awareness about drug and alcohol abuse, breast cancer, abortion, and equal rights for women into the public eye. Along with perfecting the disco dance move "the Bump" at a White House musical gala. As the wife of a Republican president.

As I said earlier, electing a woman from either party to the Oval Office will not only be a first, but a first step in a long-overdue endeavor.

How soon that happens is really up to the same kids who think of Steve McQueen as an Oscar-winning British film director.

Youth is NOT wasted on the young. That's why they can party all night and still find their cell phones in the morning.

—DR. DENIS LEARY

SIXTY IS THE NEW GO FUCK YOURSELF (or, DEAR MILLENNIALS)

Dear Millennials:

It's not what you think. I don't intend to spend this chapter tearing you a new one. And here's why. I just turned sixty and of these four things I am certain:

1. Bacon is king
2. Whoever invented apple whiskey sure as fuck ain't Irish
3. I know where my keys are, just give me a few minutes
4. You guys are the best bet America has going for it

I raised two of you. And uncled another twelve. And I'm the godfather of three. I have a lot of dogs in this race, and so far it's been a distinctly impressive experience.

I have to say that the all-American attributes of brains, brawn, sincerity, and sarcasm are being carried on with boundless ability—at least in my family. I can't spend four minutes around my nieces, nephews, son, or daughter without learning some new fact while being satirized about my sweatpants and beaten to a rebound.

There are an estimated eighty million millennials now, surpassing baby boomers as our nation's biggest age group. That's a massive swath of economic and intellectual power, energized by a proven desire to engage with peers and express opinions on a 24/7 digital basis.

I love my two children, who are now adults aged twenty-five and twenty-seven. And not just because I'm supposed to. They're funny and smart and care about what happens in the world around them. They vote and do so diligently. They speak out against racism and sexism and support gay and transgender rights. I admire their energy and am proud of their beliefs.

Do I wish they would invent a best-selling app so their mother and I could sue them for a percentage and then buy our own island somewhere?

Fuck yeah.

But I've recently given up that dream and accepted them for who they really are: part of a generation focused on making things better. Current studies prove that millennials are more socially conscious than any previous generation of Americans.

Ever.

And they are the most racially diverse, best educated, and politically active group in the history of the country. Studies also show the depth of their devotion to saving the environment and protecting the planet from impending chaos due to climate change.

And I'm with you guys on that.

Don't get me wrong—I'm not about to start counting Kleenex so you can live eight years longer. Or drive an eco-friendly car shaped like a shoe that runs on kale and unicorn sighs.

But I truly admire what you've accomplished so far and hold great hope about what you will do in the future, despite how often the critics climb all over your flaws.

My generation was labeled the Me Generation. You've been described as the triple Me Me Me Generation, with a maddening mix of polar opposite inclinations: Self-absorbed yet globally active. Allergic to books but addicted to reading your phones. Smug and terrified. I get the dichotomy and choose to cut you some slack on your softer side, because your upside is so immensely full of savvy business ideas.

You don't just use social media, you invented it. Google, Snapchat, Instagram, Twitter, Tumblr, theSkimm, Tinder, and Hinge: all created and run by millennials. As well as Dropbox, Airbnb, Pinterest, and Quora. Along with many other financial, travel, food, and entertainment apps. Plus an array of socially conscious and practically relevant products that make the world an easier place to inhabit:

Solar-energized outdoor grills
Cell phone batteries powered by walking
Cavity-fighting gum
Alzheimer patient alarm clothing
Seizure-sensitive smart watches
Solar-powered emergency lights
Disinfectant lighting systems for hospitals, laboratories, and
    the food service industry
Thermal cell phone photo printers
Portable aquaponic incubators
Affordable titanium exoskeleton and low-cost robotic hands

What did my generation invent? The apple bong. Which may have been invented even earlier, but we didn't have Google and were far too high and lazy to walk to the library and look it up. And just to be clear: we thought about inventing robotic hands. Mostly for masturbation purposes. But forgot to write the idea down.

The data so far shows that you guys vote, donate, start businesses, create jobs, and value equality in record numbers. The evidence also proves that when it comes to science, math, and technological advances you've done more in three and a half decades than any other age group.

What did my generation do? Cocaine and quaaludes. With a side order of booze.

So take my advice with a grain of blow, but take it anyways. There are a few aspects of your collective personality that could be improved upon. I know I'm painting with an incredibly broad eighty-million-strong brush, but these traits are endemic to your age, if not present in each of you:

VINYL

Listen to me: the cool sounds old records emit may soothe your musical soul for the time being, but someday soon you will have to move into an apartment or house without enough space to hold your collection of pampered paper and plastic. You may even fall in love with someone who says, "It's me or your Evan Dando on 180-gram white vinyl."

Either way, cut the cord now. Don't be a bitch to basic technology that can be easily warped, burned, or broken. Do you really want to lose all your favorite music and the countless dollars you laid down for it in a water pipe explosion? Or simply because your upstairs neighbor forgot he lit a candle?

Trust me—we waited for thousands of decades to get phones, and then another hundred and thirty years to develop ones you can walk around with while listening to music.

If you think finding, buying, carrying, caring for, and storing vinyl is better, you're probably smoking too much weed—the cleaning of which was the only thing I ever liked about vinyl in the first place. Any double album was an awesome way to separate twigs and seeds from the rest of the raw plant back in the day. Those would be the same days when the keyboard player from Yes was putting out two-disc live sets of acid-induced prog rock. The coolest sound any Rick Wakeman prog rock record ever made was the dripping hiss of its own plastic when I took a Bic lighter to my brother's copy.

I just Googled "Rick Wakeman 180 gram vinyl" and the first thing up was a copy of his twenty-seven-song 1974 double album called *Journey to the Centre of the Earth,* based on the Jules Verne science fiction novel of the same name.

Let me repeat that: twenty-seven songs. From the keyboard player in Yes. About science fiction. On 180-gram vinyl. Stop it. Stop it right now. Even if you aren't buying this shit, you started the trend. And I guarantee all twenty-seven songs sound just as endless now as they did on the day they were first released.

Sell all your inane records and get some of the money back. Before I go on a personal coast-to-coast, city-by-city meltathon.

BEARDS AND FRENCH BULLDOGS

Don't try to deny it. These two totems of millennial city life come directly from your generation. And if you feel as though I'm making you into some kind of caricature, I offer you this simple and indisputable fact: on a city block in Williamsburg, Brooklyn, I recently sat with a friend drinking coffee as we counted seventeen French bulldogs within one half hour. The owners included eleven men sporting complicated facial fuzz and some form of flannel shirt.

Lumbersexuals.

Another trend started by your age group. To look more manly, I presume. But asking one of these bulldog-toting hairy he-men to swing a hammer or change a tire might be met with a look of pure panic. Do me a favor: mix it up a little. Throw in a beagle. Maybe even a T-shirt or two. And some shaving cream.

You're starting to look like a cult.

Of macho hipsters who need to call the cops when they see a loose lug nut or German Shepherd.

Plus, we're tired of staring at egg yolk in your chin wool.

LOOK UP

Turn off your phone every once in a while and engage with the actual world instead of the digital one. There are conversations to be had face-to-face, and opinions to be expressed without using emojis or body ink.

You lead the world in nose rings, neck tats, and Distracted Walking Deaths. So many millennials get run over this way that law enforcement has a new term for you: "petextrians." I know it's a breaking-news era where every other second seems to hold a key announcement you need to be aware of, but there are more pressing and immediate concerns: like trucks and buses. Bearing down on you and your device. Smartphones can do many things, but warning you of oncoming traffic while you rage-text an ex isn't one of them.

Now, there's an idea for an app: Insta Flat. Like Candy Crush. It sends out an alarm whenever you're about to be turned into roadkill. Shit—maybe RoadKill should be the name. Keep reading while I text this idea to my kids.

Who are probably reading their phones as they cross a busy intersection right now.

UNSAFE SPACES

As evidenced by the previous entry, you're surrounded by them. Especially when you are so involved with texting and selfieing your precious life away in public places while enormous vehicles approach at Vin Diesel speed levels.

Look, the entire earth is an unsafe space. As a matter of fact, the only safe space you ever had was your mother's womb. So unless you plan on climbing back in, get ready for the real world where bad things happen all the time: death by selfie or death by disease or death by falling air-conditioning unit.

Not to mention terror attacks and mass shootings run amuck.

Your generation has grown up in a time when going to see a movie now requires 3D glasses and a grenade launcher. So I understand the desire to create a place where you can control which words, ideas, and images are allowed to enter your private environment. But let's be honest here—that ain't gonna happen. Smartphones may have an arsenal of filters that can make your waist seem thinner than Bella Thorne's, or chisel your cheekbones 'til you turn into Giselle Bündchen's brother. But it can't keep reality at bay.

You ain't Bella Thorne. Or Zac Fucking Efron. Thank God.

But look at the bright side: you are much safer than any previous generation.

Back in the sixties we found out how much life can suck right from the start. There were no car seats for kids in those days. We sat on our mothers' laps and if Dad suddenly had to jam on the brakes we bounced our heads off steel dashboards and edgy iron door handles. There weren't even any seat belts until 1968, but that didn't matter because the seats were stuffed with coal-dust foam and asbestos-coated coiled wire. If you didn't lose an eye in an accident, later on you could lose a lung just from riding around.

And bike helmets? We barely had hockey helmets. Which were essentially thin plastic lampshades with a chin strap attached. Visors and mouth guards? Those were apparently for pussies because our entire faces were just up for grabs. It was hard to complain about a few missing teeth or a detached retina when the family next door had a son ducking bullets in Vietnam and political leaders were getting their heads blown off on TV every couple of months.

What was our safe space? Sex. Until herpes showed up. And then AIDS. Both of which arrived on the scene right about the same time the first babies in your generation were born— 1980.

So I see your Safe Space and raise you two Trigger Warnings: Ann Coulter and Milo Yiannopoulos.

Regardless of their ideology and approach to expressing it, their words cannot hurt you. But refusing to let them speak does. I disagree with almost everything they have to say, but I seek out such controversial points of view so I can keep my political compass on point. You can't book a series of same-sounding liberal speakers and learn anything other than what you already know. Open the floodgates. You can only gain from the experience.

Because—as proven by Milo—sometimes when you give an asshole a microphone, he or she will end up expressing themselves right out of a job. And the media spotlight.

SAFE SPACES, UNSAFE TITLES

Wesleyan University has a dormitory named Open House that is labeled as a safe space for LGBTTQQFAGPBDSM.

These are not just really shitty letters to get in Words with Friends. They represent members of different student groups who live on campus. And a T-shirt that requires way too much reading time.

I'm hoping the FAG in the middle is an on-purpose Fuck You. Otherwise, we really should go back to the drawing board here.

The letters stand for *lesbian, gay, bisexual, transgender, transsexual, queer, questioning, flexual, asexual, genderfuck, polyamorous, bondage/discipline, dominance/submission, sadism, mascochism.*

When I was at Emerson College we just called that "the weekend."

A ton of us are with you in spirit, but please keep the letters to five. Maybe six. Once you get to seven and beyond it becomes so manic a mouthful that our modern-day ADD turns it all into politically correct mush. There are also many other iterations flying around out there, like these:

LGBTQIAPK
LGBTQQIP2SA
LGBTTQQIAAP2S

It's hard to market a series of letters that start to look like European license plates. LGBTQ+ may not have every single group represented by letter, but the plus sign implies inclusion and is much easier to brand. Not to mention remember. Especially for older people like me: men mistaken for lesbians. So if you do stick with the ultra-long version, can we add in the letters MMFL?

By the way, my kids haven't texted me back yet.

BEER AND BOOZE

Speaking of marketing, you guys have managed to take dead beer brands that my generation paid five bucks a case for and resurrect them as top-shelf bar items worth six bucks a glass. Pabst Blue Ribbon, Narragansett, and Genesee Cream Ale were part beer, part paint-thinner back in my day. Now they're cool enough to have their own hats and apparel. I actually admire your ironic sense of taste and the resilience of your livers on that front.

But when it comes to booze? You guys have a somewhat softer palate. Here's the top ten list of flavored vodkas that have been developed over the last decade or so to slake your hip young thirst:

Banana
Coconut
Kissed Caramel
Caramel Apple
Bubblegum
Cotton Candy
Whipped Cream
Peanut Butter & Jelly
Buttered Popcorn
Wedding Cake

I'm not fucking with you. They are all real. And a recent extremely positive, four-star review of Pearl's Wedding Cake

Vodka includes the line: "Very sweet and pungent, there's no bite here and no noticeable vodka character."

The vodka taster commends the vodka manufacturer for making a vodka that doesn't even remotely taste like one!

Which goes back to my twenty-year-old complaint about flavored coffee: if you don't like the taste of it but you still need some speed? Put caffeine into a Pumpkin Spice Soda. Don't ruin a perfectly good java cause you're jonesing for some Junior Mints.

I'd apply the same theory to snack-infused vodkas. The message here? Maybe you shouldn't be drinking. You should be eating vodka-infused snacks. My generation didn't invent alcoholism but we sure set some world records for it. Let your generation make a breakthrough. Fuck blackouts—you guys can have snackouts. Cook that wedding cake with some Ketel One and get fined for DUIWC. Make the cops pull you over on your way home from a movie and ask, "How many bags of popcorn did you eat tonight, sir?"

Okay—so my kids STILL haven't texted me back.

This is the iCloud of anxiety I deal with every single day. The digital gap that occurs between reaching out to my adult children and waiting for them to reach back. In that quiet air sits all the troubled territory an empty nest parent has to patrol— Where are they? HOW are they? Who are they with? What are they doing?

When they were small, each evening my wife and I could count on finding out all the amazing tiny details of their day at the dinner table. Every emotional undertow coursing through their little lives would spill out as the sun set and they were back in our eager arms. We were happy to erase every tear and fear. To cure each rash and scratch. To hold them close through fevered nights and chase the scary monsters into a star-filled sky. As they turned into teenagers, Ann and I were witness to less detail but more questions, which we happily answered. Usually over dinner. We still had them in our safety zone.

But now they exist away from us, any distance becoming so enormous that just a few hours' travel time—or even twenty city blocks—can sometimes feel as if it were an ocean.

Common sense tells me they are fine because bad news travels fast no matter what form it takes. It's not an urgent emergency call I'm waiting to answer; it's just the wish to hear their voices and read the vocal tea leaves for worry, emotional pain, or disappointment.

That radio silence is my daily agitator.

Every morning my heart aches with a desire to protect them from the arrows of love lost, friendships broken, and delicate dreams that may be dying on the vine. I used to wonder why my mom wanted me to call her more often even when I was a successful forty-year-old man, and now I know why: the job of being a parent never stops. My son may be six foot six and weigh 225 pounds, but to me he's still my lanky, firstborn foal. My daughter is a strong, smart woman full of creative energy and new ideas, but all I see is my precious little girl who needs careful protection.

Just the thought of them wandering around this treacherous planet, making their way on their own each day, would send me into a psychological tailspin if I didn't keep my mind busy with other things, like writing this book. Even as I do, the urge to drive over to their apartments and randomly check in to see if they need money or my opinion or just a long and helpful hug has to be forsaken.

It's the letting go I find hardest. But that's how this all works. It's the actual circle of life.

If only I'd realized when my kids were watching *The Lion King* six million times back in the nineties how on-point that story was going to be. I used to think it was a corny Disney cartoon that led to a daily afternoon couch nap while my kids were singing along. Now I wouldn't make it through the first four minutes without bursting into tears.

I'm slowly coming to accept that this agonizing itch to shelter and safekeep my kids will never disappear. But it is easier to manage that monster when I stand back and reckon with the tools their generation has taken out into this world. Forget the bushy beards and candy booze, the ankle tats and eye earrings. Those are just surface elements when it comes to what millennials really have to offer. You are far more technologically advanced than we ever dreamed of being. And I'm realizing now that staring down at those phones is filling you up with useful and rapid information, which you process way faster than we could at your age.

From every angle one can ogle, you guys seem to have an enormous grasp on science, math, business, and the arts. A constant flow of ingenious ideas and outstanding execution. Not to mention talent. Take my line of work, for one example. Look at the amazing pool of actors you've added to it. I'll just randomly pick letters from the alphabet:

C: Channing Tatum and Chris Pine.

E: Emma Stone and Elisabeth Moss.

G: Gyllenhaal, Glover, Garfield, and Gosling.

Jennifer Lawrence, Lin-Manuel Miranda, Lupita Nyong'o, Aubrey Plaza, Issa Rae—I can't keep going because this list would become fourteen pages long.

And when it comes to rock 'n' roll?

Dear **#OldAssholesLikeMe**:

The music millennials are making doesn't suck. You've just decided to listen with your drug-addled brain stuck in Fuck the Future mode. There are just as many great new voices arising from this generation as any previous one has offered up. Maybe more. Do they have bands that suck? Yeah, just like we did. I see their 5 Seconds of Summer and raise you one Flock of Seagulls.

For every Jonas Brother there is a Goo Goo Doll.

For each Lumineer, a member of the Dave Matthews Band.

But try these icons on for size: Kendrick, Adele, Beyoncé, and Timberlake. Gaga and Ocean and Lorde and Janelle Monáe. Tame Impala and Perfume Genius. Just a few of the many millennials making distinctive music that will fill our ears for many decades to come. So put down your 50th Anniversary Deluxe Edition Special Extra Fancy-Ass Remix of *Sgt. Pepper's* and hit play on *Lemonade* or *DAMN.* You might actually dance yourself into some newfound cognition.

There are too many other talented millennial producers, directors, writers, and players to pick out and prophesize over. And a bevy of business brains that are building everything you read/hear/watch/drive/wear/ingest to live longer, etc: Michelle Phan, Mike Krieger, Divya Nag, Mark Zuckerberg, Carly Zakin, Evan Sharp, Danielle Weisberg, Julia Hartz, Ashifi Gogo, Alexia Tsotsis, and there are so many more, but I'm tired of typing their names. Google them. Or just take my word for it: they're all smarter than we are.

We ain't turning the planet over to millennials. We're standing on land they already own.

Where the best place to see a good fight is on an airplane.

Where the EPA is now run by people who think those letters stand for Every Pipeline Available.

Where a seventy-one-year-old president acts like a seventeen-year-old spoiled brat. And gets away with it.

Like I pointed out earlier in this very book: if Trump can win, anyone can. That means you. Or someone bright and sharp and well-spoken from your generation. But as Obama said in his farewell address: get active. Stop bitching and start organizing. My generation broke the planet AND politics. Your generation can fix both. This land is literally your land. Take your eighty-million-strong army and DO something with it.

Fuck worldwide fame. Be famous locally. Really local. In your own city—for making a difference. In your own neighborhood—for making things better. In your own house—for raising a family and/or keeping a relationship together. Be remembered for changing the future and making this country even greater.

What am I going to be remembered for?

Let's be honest: probably my Oscar-nominated performance as the compassionate Sergeant Elias in Oliver Stone's powerful Vietnam epic *Platoon*. As well as my SAG Award–winning role opposite Tom Hanks in *Apollo 13*. And let's not forget the Golden Globe and Emmy I garnered for *Glee*.

But in the end, those awards mean nothing to me.

Because locally—in my house—I hope to be remembered as Devin and Jack's caring, funny, and sometimes embarrassing dad. And as my stunning wife Ann's longtime paramour. Beyond that? I don't really give a fuck.

As Julius Caesar once said, *"Veni, vidi, vici."* In my case, loosely translated to mean: "I came, I saw, I sang 'The Asshole Song.'" At least five hundred times in public.

Now go sing yours.

* * *

Okay, that was a horrible ending. Sorry. Must be karma coming back to haunt me. I had to make fun of Michael J. Fox, didn't I? Let's try this again:

Find your leaders. Don't depend on more rich, white retreads from the baby boomer generation. Choose someone smart, funny, and extraordinary. Man or woman. And don't give up until you do. There IS hope and change. It happens every four years. That's why America was invented—so that when you fall out of love with whoever's momentarily in charge, you can remove their power and say, "Take a hike, douchebag."

To echo Winston Churchill's words from earlier on: if you're going through hell, keep on going.

On the other side of the fire is a clear new day.

I've been through a lot in my six decades on this earth—including the devastating and sudden early deaths of my dad and cousin Jerry, as well as two of my closest friends. I've overcome drug and alcohol abuse, not to mention a vicious battle against scarlet fever as a child and the tremendous odds of a roller-coaster career while trying to feed and raise a family of my own. Plus, numerous health scares that almost took down my infant son, iron-willed mother, and other close relatives. Along with diseases and sickness that have taken several other cousins, aunts, and uncles from us far too early.

So, to paraphrase another old saying: what doesn't kill you not only makes you stronger, it makes you wiser and deeper and ready for more.

I'm living proof.

Now let's go kick some ass. (And get my kids to call me.)

GRATITUDES AND APPRECIATION

I could not have written this book without the dedicated help and boundless energy of several people.

Not just the many morons who populate our world with idiotic ideas and Twitter twattery. Minus their Daily Douche behavior, I would've had little inspiration to sit down and vent for 200-plus pages. Or think of an app called the Daily Douche that reports their stupidity 24/7.

So thanks to all the assholes out there.

But I also want to tribute the truly creative brains who focused on this manuscript from day one of its inception:

Jim Serpico and Eric Simonoff were vital coaches throughout the writing process, from first pitch to final product. Jim's creative acumen and business approach cleared my head and my schedule. If you're a writer and Eric isn't your agent? You're missing a lot of laughs and a ton of great advice.

Molly Stern and Tricia Boczkowski at Crown were unrelenting champions of the original premise, and fearless leaders when it came to putting this whole package together. They are also smart, funny, and a blast to work with. Which helps a lot. Tricia batted about .995 when it came to giving me great notes.

Other exceptional Crown assistance came from David Drake, Tammy Blake, and Julie Cepler. Without their urging and support, this project never gets off the ground.

My lovely assistant, Leslie Fradkin, puts up with a lot and brings even more. She's hilariously terrific.

Marisa Martins and Carrie Gordon at 42West also make me laugh when we travel the earth doing everything we can to spread the good word on whatever I'm doing. They are really great at their jobs and a lot of fun to hang out with.

My gifted friend of forty years, the novelist and comedy writer Bill Scheft remains a go-to guy for early reads and late revisions, not to mention his massive contribution to the Four Score and 7 Seconds Ago tweet section. I cannot say enough about how thankful I am to have a craftsman of Bill's caliber busting my chops. He's a first-ballot mensch. And a fellow Boston sports fan. Which counts. **#Orr4ever**

My wife, Ann, let me selfishly write into daily oblivion for months on end and graciously offered her succinct notes along with several great lines and ideas for this "book." I place that word in quotes because I not only live with someone funnier and far more intelligent than I am, but a best-selling author of actual literary acclaim.

Her talent is a wonder to witness.

Combine that with her absolute devotion to our family—plus an always available ear for my opinions and those of our two adult children—and you get the most amazing person that's ever been my honor to know. And I get to spend almost every single day in her company. She forgives my flaws while making me a better man. I couldn't write this "book"—or do anything else—without her by my side.

And finally: Jesus.

Not Jesus-the-Son-of-God Jesus. He's busy watching movies in Alabama.

No, I'm talking about Jesus Alou. Why? Because when I was a kid, he was the only real guy I knew named Jesus. The only guy in actual day-to-day life who was walking around answering to that name. But in fifteen years of Major League baseball his yearly batting average was .280 with 4 home runs and 44 RBIs. I remember thinking: *If God exists, wouldn't He want the guy named after His only son to be a kickass ballplayer who wins the Triple Crown every year?*

Guess not.

This tiny, sports-related seed of skepticism grew into an oak tree of doubt about what the nuns were teaching us. Which led to a lot of my whispered back-row sarcasm when the Religion Nun was writing on the blackboard. Which made my friends cackle. Which pissed off the nun. And only increased the snickering when she tried to suppress our laughter. Which turned me into a class clown.

So thank you, Jesus Alou.

And most final of all: I speak for every class clown of my generation when I say George Carlin was—and remains—our only fucking saint. RIP, Saint George of Morningside Heights. Your words are comedy scripture. As are those of the Reverend Richard Pryor.

Holy shit.

I think we're gonna need two more statues.

Life is too short, baseball is too long, and I hated *The Emoji Movie*. Not as much as *Operation Dumbo Drop*. But close.

—JESUS H. CHRIST, 2017